Messiah's Alphabet

Book 4
Verbs and More Grammar for Biblical Hebrew

Messiah's Alphabet

Book 4
Verbs and More Grammar for Biblical Hebrew

James T. and Lisa M. Cummins

For then will I turn to the people a pure language,
that they may all call upon the name of the LORD,
to serve him with one consent.
Zephaniah 3:9, KJV

But the goal of our instruction is love from a pure heart
and a good conscience and a sincere faith.
1 Timothy 1:5, NASB

Table Of Contents

continued, next page

Table of Contents, *continued*

continued, next page

Table of Contents, *continued*

Introduction

Welcome to Book 4 of the *Messiah's Alphabet* series in Biblical Hebrew language instruction. **Let's begin by offering thanks to our LORD, Messiah Yeshua ("Jesus") for the privilege of continuing our study of the Hebrew language. "Thank You, LORD, for having given us the ability and perseverance to bring us to this point! May we use our Hebrew knowledge to be conformed to Your image in complete obedience to You, for Your glory. Amen!"**

This book is intended for those who have completed the first, second and third workbooks of the *Messiah's Alphabet* series. Book 4 will maintain the same lighthearted spirit as the first books. It includes answer keys, puzzles, flashcards, Word Lists and all the tools you need to succeed. Remember to ask our LORD for His grace and help before each study session, and above all, rely upon His supernatural strength, for He promises that "You can do all things through Him who strengthens you" (Philippians 4:13).

To succeed with this workbook, you need to be able to easily recognize the meanings of all the Hebrew words from the Word Lists in Books 2 and 3. For a quick refresher, you can either study all your flashcards from those books, or simply review the glossary at the end of Book 3.

In Book 4, we will continue to introduce new Biblical Hebrew vocabulary as we go along from lesson to lesson. The best part about Book 4 is that you will finally have the chance to learn about Hebrew verbs. Hebrew verbs are wonderful, powerful things! You will get lots of practice reading them in actual Hebrew scripture, too.

It is our prayer that the Word of God will come into sharper focus as your knowledge of Biblical Hebrew increases. With that sharper focus will come better understanding. With that better understanding will come more complete obedience, should you choose to obey what He teaches you in scripture. What follows that obedience? Blessing upon blessing, more than you can hold. Joy, peace and contentment. What a privileged path He has laid for your feet.

"You make known to me the path of life;
in Your presence there is fullness of joy;
at Your right hand are pleasures forevermore."
– Psalm 16:11

Audio Files And Other Online Help

If you will be studying this book on your own without the help of an instructor, we strongly suggest that you download the **FREE mp3 audio files** available on our website:

www.messiahsalphabet.com

The audio files will enable you to hear the correct pronunciation of the Hebrew vocabulary introduced in this book. You will need an mp3 player, a computer, or other mp3-compatible device in order to listen to these files.

Alternatively, we have made these same audio files available for purchase as a physical audio CD through the online retailers who carry our books. Our CDs work great on most modern CD players which can read newer formats, but be aware that certain CD players (especially very old ones) may not have the capability to play them. (Note: To find our CDs, you might need to type "Messiah's Alphabet audio CD" into the vendor's search field, because, being audio CDs, they sometimes only get listed under the "music" category. The audio CDs won't always show up under the "book" category, which is where our workbooks are usually listed.)

Lesson 1:
Roots And The Past Tense

So far in the *Messiah's Alphabet* series, the only verb form we have had the opportunity to teach you is the form called the *participle*. In English, a participle is usually represented by forms ending in *ing*, such as *speaking, walking, being*. You learned how to translate the participle forms of several Hebrew verbs in Book 3, such as the Hebrew words for *loving, saying, choosing, trusting, creating, walking, remembering, forming, reigning, giving, making/doing*, and *guarding/keeping*.

Participles are great, but what about *other* tenses of Hebrew verbs? In Hebrew, how would you express the *future* tense ("the king will reign") or the *past* tense ("the king reigned")? What about the *imperative* ("Reign, O King!") or the *infinitive* ("to reign")? That's what this book will cover, lesson by lesson. We'd like to begin by teaching you about the **past tense**, right here in Lesson 1.

But, before we do that, it's important to talk about **roots.**

Roots In The English Language

Languages have a way of developing that reminds us of the way a tree grows. A small group of letters will often express a basic concept which might later "branch out" into many other words containing this same group of letters. These words will have similar or related meanings to the original group of letters. In English, we call a **"root" any group of letters which is *not* a prefix or suffix, which has its own basic meaning, and from which many related words can be formed**.

Let's look at an example. The root *dict* has the basic meaning of *to speak, to say* or *to declare*. Can you think of any words in the English language which contain this four letter spelling? Here's a short list of just a few:

<u>Dict</u>ate - to command or proclaim

<u>Dict</u>ion - language, choice of words/speech

<u>Dict</u>ionary - a collection of words (used in speech)

Contra<u>dict</u> - to "speak against" (to say the opposite)

Pre<u>dict</u> - to "speak before" (to declare something ahead of time)

Male<u>dict</u>ion - spoken words of ill will (a curse)

The powerful thing about roots is that they are not limited to a certain *type* of word. Like a spreading vine, you'll notice them creeping into all kinds of words – verbs, adjectives, nouns, and more. Once you learn how to recognize them, you'll see them everywhere:

verb: *dictate*   noun: *dictator*   adjective: *dictatorial*

verb: *predict*   noun: *prediction*   adjective: *predictive*

Roots In The Hebrew Language

Just like in English, Hebrew has its own **roots**. In fact, the entire Hebrew language is structured around its root system. **In Hebrew, a root is a set of letters** (usually three) **which expresses a basic concept.** Additional letters or certain vowels will be added to the root to make new words which "branch out" into more specific meanings that are related to the root meaning. (This is very similar to our English example on the previous page, in which the basic meaning of the root *dict* "branched out" into words with more specific meanings, just by adding letters to the root.)

Here's a **Hebrew example of root letters** from three words you will remember from your studies:

blessed (participle or verbal adjective)   בָּרוּךְ

blessing (noun)   בְּרָכָה

blessings (plural noun)   בְּרָכוֹת

Study these three Hebrew spellings carefully. **Which three letters** (consonants) **appear in all three words in the same order?** (Be careful to ignore any letters which are really acting as vowels, such as the *shoo-rook* וּ in the first word.) Below, we have enlarged the Hebrew and colored in **only the root letter consonants** so they are easier to see:

That's right; you guessed it! The only letters which are repeated in all three words above are the *bayt*, the *raysh* and the *chaf*, **in that order.** (Yes, the order matters!) These three letters make up a **Hebrew root**. Roots are often written with periods separating their letters, as shown:

בּ.ר.ךְ

You might be surprised to learn that the meaning of the root בּ.ר.ךְ is actually "to bend the knee," i.e., "to kneel." From this basic meaning we get words like "blessing," in the sense of someone *bending toward another to show honor* (a man *bending his knee* toward a superior or to God) or *inclining toward another to show favor* (as a king might do toward a favored subject).

Below is a "tree diagram" we like to use when teaching about roots. The three root letters are written over the "roots" of the tree in the picture. The basic meaning of the root is written on the "trunk," and some of the various words which "branch out" from this basic meaning are written on the "branches." **Can you recognize the root letters pervading every word?** As an additional exercise, take a few seconds and **highlight** or **circle** the three root letters in each word.

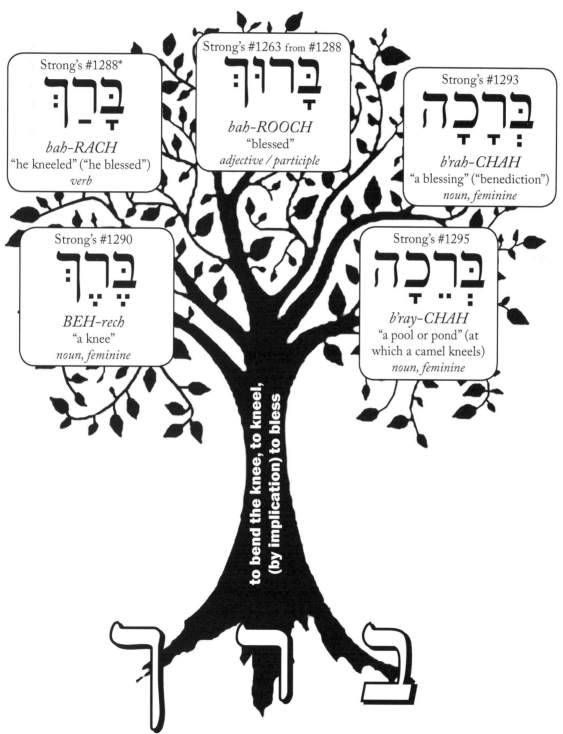

Strong's #1288*
בָּרַךְ
bah-RACH
"he kneeled" ("he blessed")
verb

Strong's #1263 *from* #1288
בָּרוּךְ
bah-ROOCH
"blessed"
adjective / participle

Strong's #1293
בְּרָכָה
b'rah-CHAH
"a blessing" ("benediction")
noun, feminine

Strong's #1290
בֶּרֶךְ
BEH-rech
"a knee"
noun, feminine

Strong's #1295
בְּרֵכָה
b'ray-CHAH
"a pool or pond" (at which a camel kneels)
noun, feminine

to bend the knee, to kneel, (by implication) to bless

ברך

* "Strong's numbers" are from a numerical index of a fabulous dictionary called *Strong's Dictionary*, which was designed just for us English speakers and contains every Hebrew and Greek word found in scripture. The numbers make it easy for anyone to look up a Hebrew or Greek word in *Strong's Dictionary*, without needing any prior knowledge of Hebrew or Greek.

The Power Of Hebrew Roots

From the example on the previous page, you probably got a sense of how powerful Hebrew roots can be. The more "root vocabulary" you can acquire, the better grasp you will have of the deeper meanings of scripture. There are literally *hundreds* of beautiful examples we could share, but on this page, we'd like to bless you with just *one*. (You don't need to memorize any of these roots right now. We just want to you "catch the fever" about the awesome power of roots!)

"He Rested" On The "Sabbath"

Ever wonder where the strange word "sabbath" *(shabbat)* really came from? Take a look at the following verse, Genesis 2:3.

in it	for	it	and made holy	the seventh	day	*direct object marker*	God	and blessed

to make	God	created	which	His work	from all	He rested

Let's take a closer look at the Hebrew verb used in the verse above for "he rested" (highlighted in gray). Now, we'll write it above the word for "sabbath" which you learned in previous books in our series:

he rested שָׁבַת

sabbath שַׁבָּת

Clearly, these two words have the same exact root letters (the letters בּ and ב are really just variations of the same letter). The root שׁ.ב.ת (Strong's #7673) means *to repose, to desist from exertion*. Therefore, it is very evident why the underlying basic meaning of the word "sabbath" is *the day of rest*.

By the way (on a different topic altogether), did you happen to notice the *first* word in the verse above for "and blessed"? Yep! It's a verb form of the root we studied on the previous page! You might have guessed its meaning even without our little definition underneath it, because its three root letters would have given it away.

Root Nomenclature

Nomenclature is just a fancy word for "a system of naming things." Notice that root nomenclature doesn't include any dots which might ordinarily be in the center of certain Hebrew letters. There aren't any vowels in root nomenclature, either. In Hebrew, there is a special term for text which has been stripped down to the bare bones of *only* the basic consonant shapes: **unpointed text.** Root nomenclature uses *unpointed text* wherever possible.

More Biblical Vocabulary

Before we dive into learning about the past tense, we will need to introduce a few new words which are prevalent in the Bible and which will appear in your exercises throughout this book. Recall that the *right* side of our Word List is where you will find the word's *singular* form, and the *left* side is where you will find its *plural* form, where applicable.

Word List: Masculine Nouns

remembrances, memorials	*zich-ro-NŌT*	mp	זִכְרוֹנוֹת	remembrance, memorial	*zih-kah-RŌN** ms	זִכָּרוֹן
prophets	*n'vee-EEM*	mp	נְבִיאִים	prophet	*nah-VEE* ms	נָבִיא
servants, slaves	*ah-vah-DEEM*	mp	עֲבָדִים	servant, slave	*EH-ved* ms	עֶבֶד
				holiness	*KŌ-desh*** ms	קֹדֶשׁ

*Note the exceptional feminine plural ending on this masculine noun. A variant of *zikaron* זִכָּרוֹן is the Hebrew word *zaycher* זֵכֶר which also means *remembrance, memorial, or memory.* Both words express much more than simply "recalling an event from the past." In scripture, they often connote the idea of *bringing God's or one's own attention to an event of spiritual significance* – whether that event exists in the past, present, future, or extends through all of time. There is a prophetic power in the act of *memorial* where it relates to holy scripture. In both the Old and New Testaments, believers are frequently commanded to "hold memorials" or "do things in remembrance."

**Note the exceptional emphasis on the *first* syllable of the word *kodesh.* A variant of the Biblical spelling of *kodesh* קֹדֶשׁ is another spelling often found in extra-biblical Hebrew writings such as modern Hebrew prayerbooks: *k'dooshah* קְדוּשָׁה – although this variant spelling happens to be a feminine noun.

Another note about the noun *kodesh:* Even though we have not listed a plural form of this noun in the Word List above, a plural form certainly does exist and appears often in your Bible. The plural spelling is *kah-dah-sheem* קָדָשִׁים, literally meaning "holinesses." This doesn't seem like a word which would come in handy at all, at least not in our modern way of speaking. However, Biblical Hebrew uses this plural form in a well-known *idiom* (figure of speech): קֹדֶשׁ קָדָשִׁים *holy of holies.* This idiom appears in Exodus 29:37, for example, where translators tend to translate this indefinite construct chain as an adjective meaning "most holy." In other places in scripture, the definite construct chain קֹדֶשׁ הַקֳּדָשִׁים *the holy of holies* is translated as a noun meaning "the most holy of holy (places)," i.e., the innermost sanctified room within the tabernacle or temple (Exodus 26:33, for example).

Word List: Feminine Nouns

	greatness*	g'doo-LAH	fs	גְּדֻלָּה
joys	s'mah-CHŌT	fp	שְׂמָחוֹת	joy, gladness	sim-CHAH	fs	שִׂמְחָה

*Does this noun feel familiar to you somehow? Perhaps you are remembering the word *gadol*, גָּדוֹל meaning "great, big" from your prior studies in our series. Do you see the root letters common to both words?

By the way, an alternate spelling of *g'doolah* גְּדֻלָּה is גְּדוּלָּה, in which the *oo* sound is represented by the *shoo-rook*.

Word List: Other Helpful Words And Phrases

no, not	lō	לֹא
forever and ever**	l'ō-LAHM vah-EHD	לְעוֹלָם וָעֶד

**Those of you who are of a religious Jewish background will recognize this familiar phrase, which appears in many songs and poems in Hebrew liturgy. Since many of you attend Messianic congregations and use the phrase in song and liturgy there, we thought it would be very helpful to add it to your vocabulary. It does appear in scripture as well – some good examples are Exodus 15:18, Psalm 9:5, Psalm 119:44, Daniel 12:3, and Micah 4:5.

Participle Review

Remember those wonderful verb forms you learned in Book 3, called *participles?* They were similiar to our English verbs ending in "ing" such as *walking, doing, creating, making.* These versatile words could even act like adjectives or nouns: *Hand me down my walking cane* (adjective). *The fun of it is in the doing* (noun). **Recall that Hebrew has four forms of every participle,** to match up with the gender and number of the person(s) that is doing the activity or the object(s) that is being described. Here are some of the participles you have already learned:

Word Table: The Four Forms Of The Participles				
	feminine plural	masculine plural	feminine singular	masculine singular
loving	אוֹהֲבוֹת	אוֹהֲבִים	אוֹהֶבֶת	אוֹהֵב
saying	אוֹמְרוֹת	אוֹמְרִים	אוֹמֶרֶת	אוֹמֵר
walking, going	הוֹלְכוֹת	הוֹלְכִים	הוֹלֶכֶת	הוֹלֵךְ
remembering	זוֹכְרוֹת	זוֹכְרִים	זוֹכֶרֶת	זוֹכֵר
giving	נוֹתְנוֹת	נוֹתְנִים	נוֹתֶנֶת	נוֹתֵן

You learned many more participles than the ones above, of course, but our purpose in having you look at this short table is to become skillful at noticing the **root consonants** that appear in every form. As an additional exercise, **please take a pencil or highlighter and circle or highlight the root letters in each of the four forms above.** Remember: You are looking for the three letters which appear in *every* form.

Are you done finding the root letters? Here are the answers:

א.ה.ב

א.מ.ר

ה.ל.ך

ז.כ.ר

נ.ת.ן

The Past Tense Pattern

Now that you really understand roots, it is finally time to learn the pattern of vowels and additional letters for the Hebrew past tense! You'll see that there are nine different forms you will need to learn to recognize. *Most* verbs will follow this pattern for the past tense (but there are, of course, some exceptions). Below, we have chosen one example, מ.ל.ך *rule, reign,* to illustrate how the past tense vowels and consonants go around the root letters. This time, we put the root letters in outline form and the pattern in black, to make the pattern stand out.

we ruled, *mah-LACH-noo,* 1cp

I ruled, *mah-LACH-tee,* 1cs or

you ruled, *m'-lach-TEM,* 2mp

you ruled, *mah-LACH-tah,* 2ms

you ruled, *m'-lach-TEN,* 2fp

you ruled, *mah-LACHT,* 2fs

they ruled, *mahl-CHOO,* 3mp

he ruled, *mah-LACH,* 3ms

they ruled, *mahl-CHOO,* 3fp

she ruled, *mahl-CHAH,* 3fs

Notes About The Pattern On The Previous Page

You might be wondering why we said you needed to memorize only **nine** forms when there are clearly **ten** different situations shown. If you look carefully at the two forms at the bottom of the left column, you'll see the Hebrew spelling is exactly the same for either the male or the female situations of "they ruled." So, you are off the hook for the tenth form!

Please note that **some of forms put the accent on the second syllable** rather than the last syllable. This will be true for all verbs in the past tense which follow this pattern. We indicate the accented syllable by writing that syllable in all capital letters. You may listen to our audio files to get a better feel for the way these words are pronounced.

About grammatical nomenclature: On the previous page, you'll see three-part codes such as "1cs" or "2mp." Recall that the number **1, 2** or **3** stands for **first** person, **second** person or **third** person. An easy technique to remember the three "persons" in grammar is to pretend you are at a party with lots of people in a huge room. Loud music is blaring. You are standing very close to a man, shouting in his ear, and asking about the identity of another person who is wearing a red hat on the opposite side of the room. You might shout this: "See that lady over there in the red hat? **I** was wondering if **you** know who **she** is." Now, repeat this sentence out loud. With each bolded word, **point** to each person in this order:

1. When you say "I," point to *yourself*. This is the grammatical *first person*.

2. When you say "you," point to the person you are speaking *to*. This is the grammatical *second person*.

3. When you say "she," point to the person you are talking *about*. This is the grammatical *third person*.

To remind yourself about the meaning of the first, second and third person in a **plural** situation, just repeat the same "pointing exercise" above, but this time, pretend that a small *group* of you at the party (maybe two or three people) are talking to a second small *group* (two or three others) about a third *group* of people wearing red hats on the opposite side of the room. This time, you might holler the following: "See those people over there in the red hats? **We** were wondering if **you guys** know who **they** are." In this situation, "we" is the *first person*, "you" (i.e., "you guys" or "you, plural") is the *second person*, and "they" is the *third person*.

Of course, in our three-part codes on the previous page, the letter abbreviations are obvious. The letter *m* or *f* stands for *male* or *female*, while the letter *c* stands for *common* (either male or female, or perhaps both male and female). The letter *s* stands for *singular*, and *p* stands for *plural*.

Why do we harp so much about learning this grammatical nomenclature? The reason is that **all Hebrew language books, Bible language reference tools, dictionaries and verb tables use codes like these** (or some very similar variation of them). We want you to be able to recognize and understand them, no matter which Biblical reference tool you decide to use in the future. (Most textbooks don't use the little "man" and "woman" icons which we use in our series; they only use codes.) So, in our books, from this point forward, we will try to include these codes wherever applicable.

Other Methods Of Displaying Patterns

A compact and easy way of displaying verb patterns is to simply use three X's to stand for the root letters. (Many textbooks use this technique.) For example, the past tense pattern we just taught would look like this:

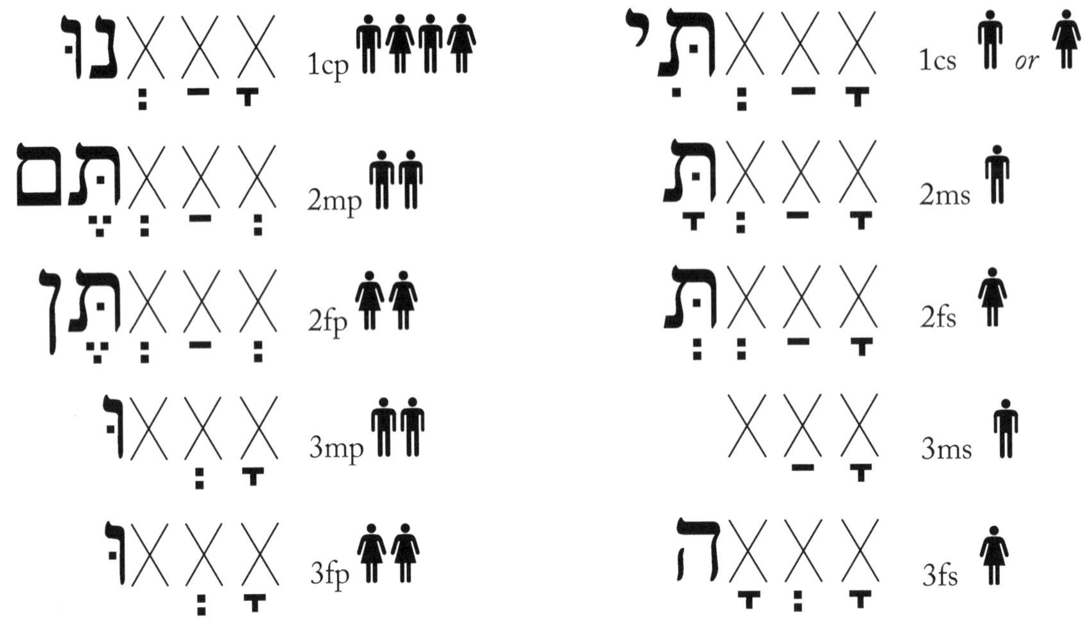

נוּXXX	1cp	תִּיXXX	1cs
תֶּםXXX	2mp	תָּXXX	2ms
תֶּןXXX	2fp	תְּXXX	2fs
וּXXX	3mp	XXX	3ms
וּXXX	3fp	הXXX	3fs

Some textbooks will choose *not* to use the grammar codes above. Instead, they will actually take the time to show the Hebrew pronouns which go with each verb form! This can be *very* handy and can save a lot of time for you. Here's how those textbooks do it:

אֲנַחְנוּ נוּXXX		אֲנִי תִּיXXX	
אַתֶּם תֶּםXXX		אַתָּה תָּXXX	
אַתֶּן תֶּןXXX		אַתְּ תְּXXX	
הֵם וּXXX		הוּא XXX	
הֵן וּXXX		הִיא הXXX	

There are two advantages to this type of display. One is that it provides a ready-made list of two-word Hebrew sentences, each having a pronoun and verb. The other is that you can easily see the similarities between some of the pronouns and the verb suffixes. All four of the pronouns which mean *you*, for example, have suffixes in their verbs which match or rhyme with their pronouns.

Using The Past Tense Pattern To *Conjugate* A Verb

The term **to conjugate** is a fancy grammar term which means **to give the different forms of a verb as they vary according to voice, mood, tense, number, gender and person.** In the particular case of our simple past tense pattern, its conjugation is affected only by *number, gender* and *person* right now. (Don't worry about voice and mood at this time; those are topics for later.)

An example of a **conjugated** verb is on page 20. We would say that, on that page, we have "**conjugated** the Hebrew verb *rule, reign* in the past tense." Very simply, this means we have listed all the different forms of this verb in the past tense as they vary according to the *number, gender* and *person* of the subject(s) who did the ruling or reigning.

Let's use our past tense pattern with a new verb. We will once again show the past tense pattern with the three X's, and we will then insert the root letters for the verb we want to conjugate in the past tense. Let's try this right now, using the root letters שׁ.מ.ר *guard, keep.*

The Past Tense Pattern

אֲנַחְנוּ XXX־נוּ   אֲנִי XXX־תִּי

אַתֶּם XXX־תֶּם   אַתָּה XXX־תָּ

אַתֶּן XXX־תֶּן   אַתְּ XXX־תְּ

הֵם XXX־וּ   הוּא XXX

הֵן XXX־וּ   הִיא XXX־ה

The Verb שׁ.מ.ר Conjugated In The Past Tense

Take a blank sheet of notebook paper and write the past tense pattern above, inserting the three root letters for the Hebrew verb *guard, keep* in place of the X's. Its conjugation should look like:

we guarded	אֲנַחְנוּ שָׁמַרְנוּ	I guarded	אֲנִי שָׁמַרְתִּי
you *(mp)* guarded	אַתֶּם שְׁמַרְתֶּם	you *(ms)* guarded	אַתָּה שָׁמַרְתָּ
you *(fp)* guarded	אַתֶּן שְׁמַרְתֶּן	you *(fs)* guarded	אַתְּ שָׁמַרְתְּ
they *(m)* guarded	הֵם שָׁמְרוּ	he guarded	הוּא שָׁמַר
they *(f)* guarded	הֵן שָׁמְרוּ	she guarded	הִיא שָׁמְרָה

Exercise 1.1 - Conjugation Practice

Conjugate the following verb, meaning *remember, recall,* by filling in the blanks. Then write the translation of each phrase. An example has already been done for you. Indicate the number and gender where necessary in your English translations. Make sure to read each Hebrew phrase out loud, to teach yourself the pronunciation. Answers are at the bottom.

⑥ אֲנַחְנוּ _____ _____

⑦ אַתֶּם _____ _____

⑧ אַתֶּן _____ _____

⑨ הֵם _____ _____

⑩ הֵן _____ _____

① אֲנִי זָכַרְתִּי _____ I remembered

② אַתָּה _____ _____

③ אַתְּ _____ _____

④ הוּא _____ _____

⑤ הִיא _____ _____

Answers 1.1 - Conjugation Practice

⑥ אֲנַחְנוּ זָכַרְנוּ — we remembered*

⑦ אַתֶּם זְכַרְתֶּם — you (mp) remembered

⑧ אַתֶּן זְכַרְתֶּן — you (fp) remembered

⑨ הֵם זָכְרוּ — they (m) remembered

⑩ הֵן זָכְרוּ — they (f) remembered

① אֲנִי זָכַרְתִּי — I remembered*

② אַתָּה זָכַרְתָּ — you (ms) remembered*

③ אַתְּ זָכַרְתְּ — you (fs) remembered

④ הוּא זָכַר — he remembered

⑤ הִיא זָכְרָה — she remembered

*Pronunciation notes: All of the verb forms in this conjugation are pronounced as usual with the accent on the *last* syllable, with the following exceptions, in which the accent is on the *second* syllable.

1cs form is pronounced *zah-CHAR-tee*
2ms form is pronounced *zah-CHAR-tah*
1cp form is pronouned *zah-CHAR-noo*

These exceptional accents will apply to all verbs which follow this pattern.

Slightly Exceptional Spellings

On this page, we have displayed the **conjugated past tenses** of other verbs which follow the pattern closely, but with minor differences in some of the vowels. **We have highlighted any exceptional vowels in gray**, but you will be happy to see that these differences really are trivial. You don't have to memorize these slight differences. Right now, your only goal should be to **learn to recognize each form and translate it correctly into English.**

א.מ.ר *say*

אָמַרְנוּ	1cp	אָמַרְתִּי	1cs
אֲמַרְתֶּם	2mp	אָמַרְתָּ	2ms
אֲמַרְתֶּן	2fp	אָמַרְתְּ	2fs
אָמְרוּ	3mp	אָמַר	3ms
אָמְרוּ	3fp	אָמְרָה	3fs

א.ה.ב *love*

אָהַבְנוּ	1cp	אָהַבְתִּי	1cs
אֲהַבְתֶּם	2mp	אָהַבְתָּ	2ms
אֲהַבְתֶּן	2fp	אָהַבְתְּ	2fs
אָהֲבוּ	3mp	אָהַב	3ms
אָהֲבוּ	3fp	אָהֲבָה	3fs

ב.ט.ח *trust*

בָּטַחְנוּ	1cp	בָּטַחְתִּי	1cs
בְּטַחְתֶּם	2mp	בָּטַחְתָּ	2ms
בְּטַחְתֶּן	2fp	בָּטַחַתְּ	2fs
בָּטְחוּ	3mp	בָּטַח	3ms
בָּטְחוּ	3fp	בָּטְחָה	3fs

The second syllable is also stressed on this verb's 2fs form.

ב.ח.ר *choose*

בָּחַרְנוּ	1cp	בָּחַרְתִּי	1cs
בְּחַרְתֶּם	2mp	בָּחַרְתָּ	2ms
בְּחַרְתֶּן	2fp	בָּחַרְתְּ	2fs
בָּחֲרוּ	3mp	בָּחַר	3ms
בָּחֲרוּ	3fp	בָּחֲרָה	3fs

ה.ל.ך *walk, go*

הָלַכְנוּ	1cp	הָלַכְתִּי	1cs
הֲלַכְתֶּם	2mp	הָלַכְתָּ	2ms
הֲלַכְתֶּן	2fp	הָלַכְתְּ	2fs
הָלְכוּ	3mp	הָלַךְ	3ms
הָלְכוּ	3fp	הָלְכָה	3fs

The forms on this page represent the *past tense*. As you practice reading this page out loud, you should also translate each meaning out loud. For example, in the verb *walk* at right, start at the top of the right column and go down the column, saying out loud, "*ha-LACH-tee:* I walked. *ha-LACH-tah:* you walked," etc.

As you pronounce each of these patterns out loud, you'll understand why some of the vowels were changed in these exceptional spellings. If the original pattern vowels were forced onto *every* verb without exception, some verb forms would become awkward to pronounce.

Different Ways To Translate The Hebrew Past Tense

Did you notice on the previous page that we left all the pronouns off the lists? All we had was the verb form. The neat thing about Hebrew verbs is that **the pronoun meaning is actually included within each verb form!**

Let's say you want to write a very short sentence, "I remembered." You can write it two ways:

אֲנִי זָכַרְתִּי.

I remembered.

OR

זָכַרְתִּי.

I remembered.

That's right! **The two sentences above have identical meaning.** Did you ever in your life think you could write a one-word sentence? Well, in Hebrew, it is possible!

While we're talking about meanings, let's talk about how flexible the Hebrew past tense can be. In English, we are required to use extra little words called *helping verbs* to show different shades of meaning in the past tense.

For example, if you were proud that you did not forget to get milk at the store, you might boast, "I remembered to get milk!" This is a simple, straightforward meaning of the past tense. An event happened, and it is now done and over with. No helping verbs needed here.

But, what if you need to express additional meaning? Let's say you wanted to tell why you turned your car around and headed back to the store only five minutes after you had left the parking lot to head back home. You might say, "I had remembered I also needed eggs." This sentence has a helping verb, *had*, which adds a slightly different shade of meaning.

Maybe one day at work, during a big, important meeting, your eyes are glazed and you have a dreamy smile on your face. It is obvious to everyone that you are not paying attention to the meeting. A coworker notices and whispers, "What were you just thinking about?" You might whisper back, "Oh... I was remembering what a lovely time I had on my vacation in the Bahamas last week." The helping verb in this sentence is the word *was*.

Hebrew does not use helping verbs, yet the Hebrew past tense contains many possible shades of meaning. It's up to you, as the translator, to read the context carefully and insert any helping verbs into your English translations that you feel are necessary to express the true meaning of the passage. Here are some possible sentence translations for the Hebrew verb *I remembered*:

זָכַרְתִּי   *can mean...*

I remembered.

I had remembered.

I did remember.

I was remembering.

I have remembered.

More Exceptional Spellings

There are two other verbs you encountered in other books in our series. We waited until the end of this lesson to teach you their past tense forms, because their spellings are even more exceptional than the last set. These are the verbs *give* and *make/do*. They are so strange that they don't even use all three of their root letters in the pattern. Some textbooks won't even show you all the forms for these verbs because they are (1) so weird looking, and (2) many of the forms hardly get used in the Bible. The vast majority of the times these verbs are used in scripture, they will appear in 1cs, 2ms, 3ms, or 3mp forms, because the subjects doing these verbs are usually God, a man, or a group of men. So, please don't attempt to memorize all these exceptional spellings. Just be able to recognize the past tense forms when you see them, especially focusing on the 1cs, 2ms, 3ms and 3mp forms.

עָ.שֹׁ.ה *make, do**

עָשִׂינוּ	*1cp*	עָשִׂיתִי	*1cs*
עֲשִׂיתֶם	*2mp*	עָשִׂיתָ	*2ms*
עֲשִׂיתֶן	*2fp*	עָשִׂית	*2fs*
עָשׂוּ	*3mp*	עָשָׂה	*3ms*
עָשׂוּ	*3fp*	עָשְׂתָה	*3fs*

נ.ת.ן *give*

נָתַנּוּ	*1cp*	נָתַתִּי	*1cs*
נְתַתֶּם	*2mp*	נָתַתָּ	*2ms*
נְתַתֶּן	*2fp*	נָתַתְּ	*2fs*
נָתְנוּ	*3mp*	נָתַן	*3ms*
נָתְנוּ	*3fp*	נָתְנָה	*3fs*

*Note the <u>pointed</u> *seen* in the root notation of this verb. When forced to differentiate between *seen* and *sheen*, grammarians will relent and will include this one tiny dot, even though the general rule is to use <u>unpointed</u> text in root nomenclature.

Like other past tense verbs, both of the verbs on this page have certain forms with exceptional accents in their pronunciation. Place the emphasis on the *second syllable* when pronouncing the 1cs, 2ms and 1cp forms. On all other forms, emphasize the *last syllable*, as usual.

The Word לֹא

The word לֹא *lo* is a **negator**. A **negator** expresses the meaning of *no* or *not*. This Hebrew word can be used in a noun sentence, or it can be placed directly in front of a verb (either past or future tense). Here are some examples of how this useful Hebrew word may appear in sentences:

David is not a big man.

דָּוִד לֹא אִישׁ גָּדוֹל.

They did not keep watch over the house.

הֵם לֹא שָׁמְרוּ עַל הַבַּיִת.

The king did not trust in God.

הַמֶּלֶךְ לֹא בָּטַח בֵּאלֹהִים.

Exercise 1.2 - Translation Practice

Translate each past tense verb form into English, then indicate its person, gender and number using the three-part grammar codes as shown in the first example.

⑥ אָהַב	_____	① הָלַכְתְּ	you walked 2fs
⑦ זְכַרְתֶּם	_____	② שָׁמַרְתִּי	_____
⑧ אָמַרְתָּ	_____	③ בָּטְחוּ	_____
⑨ נְתַתֶּן	_____	④ בָּחֲרָה	_____
⑩ עָשִׂיתִי	_____	⑤ מָלַכְנוּ	_____

Answers 1.2 - Translation Practice

⑥ אָהַב	he loved 3ms	① הָלַכְתְּ	you walked 2fs
⑦ זְכַרְתֶּם	you remembered 2mp	② שָׁמַרְתִּי	I guarded 1cs
⑧ אָמַרְתָּ	you said 2ms	③ בָּטְחוּ	they trusted 3mp/3fp
⑨ נְתַתֶּן	you gave 2fp	④ בָּחֲרָה	she chose 3fs
⑩ עָשִׂיתִי	I made 1cs	⑤ מָלַכְנוּ	we ruled 1cp

Exercise 1.3 - Conjugation Practice

On a piece of notebook paper, write all ten forms for each of the following verbs in the past tense. Translate each form into English. Feel free to refer to the lists within the lesson.

א.ה.ב	ב.ח.ר	ה.ל.ך	מ.ל.ך	שׁ.מ.ר
א.מ.ר	ב.ט.ח	ז.כ.ר	נ.ת.ן	ע.שׂ.ה

Exercise 1.4 - Riddle Review

Match each phrase or sentence to its translation, then write its circled "code letter" in the space provided. The circled letters will spell the answer to the riddle.

What's the first thing Adam and Eve did after being expelled from the garden?

Ⓛ	יֵשׁוּעַ אָמַר דְּבָרִים טוֹבִים.	We have loved holiness. ⚪
Ⓓ	הַנָּבִיא זָכַר הַתּוֹרָה.	I ruled over the peoples. ⚪
Ⓡ	הַמֶּלֶךְ לֹא שָׁמַר הָעֲבָדִים.	You gave bread. ⚪
Ⓣ	אָהַבְנוּ קֹדֶשׁ.	Yeshua has guarded over you with joy. ⚪
Ⓔ	אַתָּה נָתַתָּ לֶחֶם.	The king did not guard the servants. Ⓡ
Ⓐ	לֹא בָּטַחְנוּ בְּאַנְשֵׁי מִצְרַיִם.	You kept a memorial. ⚪
Ⓘ	הָלְכוּ אֶל בֵּית הַמֶּלֶךְ.	We did not trust the men of Egypt. ⚪
Ⓗ	מָלַכְתִּי עַל הָעַמִּים.	Yeshua said good words. ⚪
Ⓔ	הָאֵם שָׁמְרָה עַל קְדֻשַּׁת הַשַּׁבָּת.	Yeshua has chosen you. ⚪
Ⓛ	יֵשׁוּעַ בָּחַר בָּךְ.	You have given kindness. ⚪
Ⓨ	יֵשׁוּעַ שָׁמַר עָלֶיךָ בְּשִׂמְחָה.	You said. ⚪
Ⓨ	נָתַתָּ חֶסֶד.	I have loved. ⚪
Ⓘ	זִכְרוּ לְעוֹלָם וָעֶד.	They walked to the king's house. ⚪
Ⓔ	שְׁמַרְתֶּם זִכָּרוֹן.	The daughters trusted. ⚪
Ⓝ	הַמְּלָכִים נָתְנוּ.	The mother kept the holiness of the sabbath. ⚪
Ⓐ	אֲנִי אָהַבְתִּי.	The prophet remembered the law. ⚪
Ⓢ	הַבָּנוֹת בָּטְחוּ.	He walked. ⚪
Ⓡ	אַתֶּם אֲמַרְתֶּם.	They ruled. ⚪
Ⓒ	הָלַךְ.	They remembered forever and ever. ⚪
Ⓐ	מָלְכוּ.	The kings gave. ⚪

Answer: They really raised Cain.

Exercise 1.5 - Let's Read Scripture!

For each of the following scriptures, please write the translation of each word in the blank provided underneath it. We have already filled in any new words which we have not yet introduced to you. You might discover that you need a refresher on some of the possessive suffixes or construct forms which you learned in our earlier books. If you need to refer to your old books frequently, please don't be alarmed. It's just the normal, "three-steps-forward, two-steps-back" process of learning Hebrew (or any foreign language). Don't be shy, either, about using the glossary at the back of the book, if you need it. To check your answers in this exercise, see the translation provided below each scripture.

① כִּי זָכַר אֶת דְּבַר קָדְשׁוֹ אֶת אַבְרָהָם עַבְדּוֹ.

for _____ _____ *direct object marker* _____ *direct object marker* _____ _____

Translation: "For He remembered His holy word and Abraham His servant."
Literal Translation: "For he remembered the word of his holiness [and] Abraham his servant."
Context: The psalmist praises God for delivering Israel out of Egypt (Psalm 105:42).

② ...כִּי אַתֶּם בְּחַרְתֶּם לָכֶם אֶת יהוה לַעֲבֹד אוֹתוֹ...

for _____ _____ _____ *direct object marker* YHVH to serve him

Translation: "...for you have chosen to serve the Lord..."
Literal Translation: "...for you have chosen for yourselves the Lord, to serve Him..."
Context: Joshua confronts the people about their idolatry. They then promise to forsake their idols and serve God (Joshua 24:22).

③ גַּם הִיא לַגֹּלָה, הָלְכָה בַשֶּׁבִי...

yet _____ was carried away _____ into captivity

Translation: "Yet she became an exile; she went into captivity..."
Literal Translation: "Yet she was carried away; she walked into captivity..."
Context: The Lord describes how Thebes could not stand against His judgment (Nahum 3:10).

Exercise 1.5: Let's Read Scripture, *continued*

④ ...אָמַרְנוּ לַמֶּלֶךְ לֵאמֹר יַד אֱלֹהֵינוּ עַל כָּל

   ___   ____   _____   ____   saying   _____   _____

מְבַקְשָׁיו לְטוֹבָה...

_____   those who seek him

Translation: "...we had spoken to the king, saying, 'The hand of our God is upon all who seek Him for good'..."

Context: Ezra explains why he did not ask the king for soldiers or horsemen to protect him and the families of exiles on their journey back to Jerusalem (Ezra 8:22).

⑤ אָהַבְתָּ רָע מִטּוֹב, שֶׁקֶר מִדַּבֵּר צֶדֶק...

   righteousness   than to speak   lying   _____ * _____   _____

Translation: "You have loved evil more than good, lying more than to speak righteousness..."

*Note: The prefix מ, literally meaning *from*, can also be a Hebraism for *more than*.

Context: David's psalm speaks to the wicked man and warns him of his end (Psalm 52:3).

⑥ וּבְנֵי יִשְׂרָאֵל הָלְכוּ בַיַּבָּשָׁה בְּתוֹךְ הַיָּם...

   the sea   in the middle of   on dry land   _____   _____   _____

Translation: "and the sons of Israel walked on dry land in the middle of the sea..."

Context: God parts the sea to enable Israel to escape the Egyptians (Exodus 14:29).

⑦ ...בָטַחְתִּי בְחֶסֶד אֱלֹהִים עוֹלָם וָעֶד.

   _____ * _____   _____   _____

Translation: "...I have trusted in the mercy of God forever and ever."

*Note: Occasionally the term לְעוֹלָם וָעֶד appears without the prepositional prefix ל.

Context: David declares that he will prosper because he has always trusted in God (Psalm 52:8).

Lesson 1 Flashcards

Please carefully tear out the flashcard pages and cut out the flashcards. Be sure to quiz yourself using these flashcards (in random order) a few minutes every day until you know them by heart. We suggest that you pronounce each of the nine forms out loud, followed by its translation: "*Ah-HAHV-tee*, I loved. *Ah-HAHV-tah*, you loved - masculine singular. *Ah-HAHVT*, you loved - feminine singular," etc.

אֲהַבְתֶּם	אָהַב	אָהַבְתִּי	אֲמַרְתֶּם	אָמַר	אָמַרְתִּי
אֲהַבְתֶּן	אָהֲבָה	אָהַבְתָּ	אֲמַרְתֶּן	אָמְרָה	אָמַרְתָּ
אָהֲבוּ	אָהַבְנוּ	אָהַבְתְּ	אָמְרוּ	אָמַרְנוּ	אָמַרְתְּ

בְּחַרְתֶּם	בָּחַר	בָּחַרְתִּי	בְּטַחְתֶּם	בָּטַח	בָּטַחְתִּי
בְּחַרְתֶּן	בָּחֲרָה	בָּחַרְתָּ	בְּטַחְתֶּן	בָּטְחָה	בָּטַחְתָּ
בָּחֲרוּ	בָּחַרְנוּ	בָּחַרְתְּ	בָּטְחוּ	בָּטַחְנוּ	בָּטַחַתְּ

הֲלַכְתֶּם	הָלַךְ	הָלַכְתִּי	זְכַרְתֶּם	זָכַר	זָכַרְתִּי
הֲלַכְתֶּן	הָלְכָה	הָלַכְתָּ	זְכַרְתֶּן	זָכְרָה	זָכַרְתָּ
הָלְכוּ	הָלַכְנוּ	הָלַכְתְּ	זָכְרוּ	זָכַרְנוּ	זָכַרְתְּ

מְלַכְתֶּם	מָלַךְ	מָלַכְתִּי	נְתַתֶּם	נָתַן	נָתַתִּי
מְלַכְתֶּן	מָלְכָה	מָלַכְתָּ	נְתַתֶּן	נָתְנָה	נָתַתָּ
מָלְכוּ	מָלַכְנוּ	מָלַכְתְּ	נָתְנוּ	נָתַנּוּ	נָתַתְּ

Please recall that there are many other possible translations for these past tenses, which are not shown here. For example, the past tense "loved" could just as well be translated *had loved, has loved, did love, was loving*, etc. Due to limited space, we only included the most simple translation of each.

ah-hahv-TEM "you loved" (2mp)	*ah-HAHV* "he loved" (3ms)	*ah-HAHV-tee* "I loved" (1cs)	*ah-mar-TEM* "you said" (2mp)	*ah-MAR* "he said" (3ms)	*ah-MAR-tee* "I said" (1cs)
ah-hahv-TEN "you loved" (2fp)	*ah-hah-VAH* "she loved" (3fs)	*ah-HAHV-tah* "you loved" (2ms)	*ah-mar-TEN* "you said" (2fp)	*ahm-RAH* "she said" (3fs)	*ah-MAR-tah* "you said" (2ms)
ah-hah-VOO "they loved" (3cp)	*ah-HAHV-noo* "we loved" (1cp)	*ah-HAHVT* "you loved" (2fs)	*ahm-ROO* "they said" (3cp)	*ah-MAR-noo* "we said" (1cp)	*ah-MART* "you said" (2fs)
(This word was introduced in Book 4, Lesson 1)			(This word was introduced in Book 4, Lesson 1)		
b'-char-TEM "you chose" (2mp)	*bah-CHAR* "he chose" (3ms)	*bah-CHAR-tee* "I chose" (1cs)	*b'-tach-TEM* "you trusted" (2mp)	*bah-TACH* "he trusted" (3ms)	*bah-TACH-tee* "I trusted" (1cs)
b'-char-TEN "you chose" (2fp)	*bah-chah-RAH* "she chose" (3fs)	*bah-CHAR-tah* "you chose" (2ms)	*b'-tach-TEN* "you trusted" (2fp)	*baht-CHAH* "she trusted" (3fs)	*bah-TACH-tah* "you trusted" (2ms)
bach-ROO "they chose" (3cp)	*bah-CHAR-noo* "we chose" (1cp)	*bah-CHART* "you chose" (2fs)	*baht-CHOO* "they trusted" (3cp)	*bah-TACH-noo* "we trusted" (1cp)	*bah-TAH-chat* "you trusted" (2fs)
(This word was introduced in Book 4, Lesson 1)			(This word was introduced in Book 4, Lesson 1)		
hah-lach-TEM "you walked" (2mp)	*hah-LACH* "he walked" (3ms)	*hah-LACH-tee* "I walked" (1cs)	*z'-char-TEM* "you remembered" (2mp)	*zah-CHAR* "he remembered" (3ms)	*zah-CHAR-tee* "I remembered" (1cs)
hah-lach-TEN "you walked" (2fp)	*hal-CHAH* "she walked" (3fs)	*hah-LACH-tah* "you walked" (2ms)	*z'-char-TEN* "you remembered" (2fp)	*zach-RAH* "she remembered" (3fs)	*zah-CHAR-tah* "you remembered" (2ms)
hal-CHOO "they walked" (3cp)	*hah-LACH-noo* "we walked" (1cp)	*hah-LACHT* "you walked" (2fs)	*zach-ROO* "they remembered" (3cp)	*zah-CHAR-noo* "we remembered" (1cp)	*zah-CHART* "you remembered" (2fs)
(This word was introduced in Book 4, Lesson 1)			(This word was introduced in Book 4, Lesson 1)		
m'-lach-TEM "you ruled" (2mp)	*mah-LACH* "he ruled" (3ms)	*mah-LACH-tee* "I ruled" (1cs)	*n'-tah-TEM* "you gave" (2mp)	*nah-TAHN* "he gave" (3ms)	*nah-TAH-tee* "I gave" (1cs)
m'-lach-TEN "you ruled" (2fp)	*mal-CHAH* "she ruled" (3fs)	*mah-LACH-tah* "you ruled" (2ms)	*n'-tah-TEN* "you gave" (2fp)	*naht-NAH* "she gave" (3fs)	*nah-TAH-tah* "you gave" (2ms)
mal-CHOO "they ruled" (3cp)	*mah-LACH-noo* "we ruled" (1cp)	*mah-LACHT* "you ruled" (2fs)	*naht-NOO* "they gave" (3cp)	*nah-TAH-noo* "we gave" (1cp)	*nah-TAHT* "you gave" (2fs)
(This word was introduced in Book 4, Lesson 1)			(This word was introduced in Book 4, Lesson 1)		

עֲשִׂיתֶם עָשָׂה עָשִׂיתִי עֲשִׂיתֶן עָשְׂתָה עָשִׂיתָ עָשׂוּ עָשִׂינוּ עָשִׂית	שְׁמַרְתֶּם שָׁמַר שָׁמַרְתִּי שְׁמַרְתֶּן שָׁמְרָה שָׁמַרְתְּ שָׁמְרוּ שָׁמַרְנוּ שָׁמַרְתְּ
זִכָּרוֹן	נָבִיא
עֶבֶד	קֹדֶשׁ
גָּדְלָה	שִׂמְחָה
לֹא	לְעוֹלָם וָעֶד

ah-see-TEM "you made" (2mp)	*ah-SAH* "he made" (3ms)	*ah-SEE-tee* "I made" (1cs)	*sh'-mar-TEM* "you guarded" (2mp)	*shah-MAR* "he guarded" (3ms)	*shah-MAR-tee* "I guarded" (1cs)
ah-see-TEN "you made" (2fp)	*ahs-TAH* "she made" (3fs)	*ah-SEE-tah* "you made" (2ms)	*sh'-mar-TEN* "you guarded" (2fp)	*shahm-RAH* "she guarded" (3fs)	*shah-MAR-tah* "you guarded" (2ms)
ah-SOO "they made" (3cp)	*ah-SEE-noo* "we made" (1cp)	*ah-SEET* "you made" (2fs)	*shahm-ROO* "they guarded" (3cp)	*shah-MAR-noo* "we guarded" (1cp)	*shah-MART* "you guarded" (2fs)

*or, "I did," "you did," "he did," etc.
(This word was introduced in Book 4, Lesson 1)

(This word was introduced in Book 4, Lesson 1)

zih-kah-RŌN
memorial
noun, masculine, singular

(This word was introduced in Book 4, Lesson 1)

nah-VEE
prophet
noun, masculine, singular

(This word was introduced in Book 4, Lesson 1)

EH-ved
servant, slave
noun, masculine, singular

(This word was introduced in Book 4, Lesson 1)

KŌ-desh
holiness
noun, masculine, singular

(This word was introduced in Book 4, Lesson 1)

g'doo-LAH
greatness
noun, feminine, singular

(This word was introduced in Book 4, Lesson 1)

sim-CHAH
joy, gladness
noun, feminine, singular

(This word was introduced in Book 4, Lesson 1)

lō
no, not
negator

(This word was introduced in Book 4, Lesson 1)

l' ō-LAHM vah-ED
forever and ever

(This word was introduced in Book 4, Lesson 1)

Lesson 2: The Word אֶת

Perhaps you have noticed in our "Let's Read Scripture" exercises a peculiar little word that we never define for you. Instead, we write the words *direct object marker* underneath it. This is the word אֶת which rhymes with "get" or "pet." In this lesson, we will explain its unique function.

Before we do, you will need to acquire some new vocabulary. Please study the Word Lists below.

Word List: Masculine Nouns

books, documents	s'fah-REEM	mp	סְפָרִים	book, document	SAY-fehr*	ms	סֵפֶר
				voice, sound**	kōhl	ms	קוֹל
gates	sh'-ah-REEM	mp	שְׁעָרִים	gate	shah-AR	ms	שַׁעַר

*Note the emphasis on the first syllable in this word. This word technically means "book" but is often translated "scroll" in English Bibles.

**Note that there is not a plural form for this Hebrew word for "voice" or "sound." In scripture, if a whole group of people shout something, it is translated "the voice of the people," as though they all made a singular "sound."

Word List: Verbs

write	כ.ת.ב
hear	שׁ.מ.ע

From now on, we'll only list the root letters of new verbs. Once you know the three root letters for a new verb, you can just follow the regular patterns to figure out the past tense or participle forms. If there are any exceptions, we will let you know and provide you with those special spellings. For example, the verb "hear" does vary somewhat from the normal pattern in its present participle forms, *hearing*, so here they all are:

שׁוֹמְעוֹת   שׁוֹמְעִים   שׁוֹמַעַת   שׁוֹמֵעַ

fp   *mp*   *fs*   *ms*

This verb does follow the usual patterns for the past tense, thankfully, so you can write those out on your own.

which, who, that*	ah-SHEHR, sheh–	אֲשֶׁר, שֶׁ־
direct object marker	eht, ayt	אֶת, אֵת
because, that*	kee	כִּי

*A few notes about the above words:

אֲשֶׁר is *not* used as a question (which? who?), but rather as a pronoun which begins a clause that often describes a noun introduced earlier in the sentence. English examples are: "This is the man *who* saved my life." "The kind of movie I prefer is one *which* teaches a good lesson." "Good words are those *that* speak kindness." The short form of אֲשֶׁר is the prefix שֶׁ־ which has the same meaning.

The *direct object marker* has two alternate spellings and pronunciations, *eht* or *ayt*. The *eht* spelling is more common. This word will be the main focus of this lesson.

The word כִּי which means *because* or *that* may also be translated *for*. It usually acts as a conjunction. English examples of its meaning are: "And God saw the light, *that* it was good." "And God blessed the seventh day and sanctified it, *because* in it He rested." "The dove returned to the ark, *for* the waters were upon the face of the earth." This versatile Hebrew word may also be translated *when, inasmuch, indeed, though, whereas,* or many other meanings, all depending on the context of the verse.

The Direct Object In English

It's worth taking a moment here to remind ourselves what a *direct object* is, because it's the whole reason Hebrew has that special word אֵת which is a *direct object marker*.

A direct object is any noun or pronoun which receives the action of the verb in the sentence. To begin, let's look at some English examples of sentences which contain only subjects and verbs (no direct objects).

> I wrote.

> Abraham loved.

> We heard.

Each of the above sentences has a *subject* (the person doing the activity) and a *verb* (the word which describes the action). However, none of these sentences has a *direct object* (the person or thing upon which the verb is acting). Let's modify the sentences so that they have a **direct object**:

> I wrote a book.

> Abraham loved children.

> We heard a voice.

Think of the direct object as the answer to the questions "What?" or "Whom?" Whenever you are trying to figure out the direct object of a sentence, just restate the subject and verb and add the word *what?* or *whom?* to form a question. Answer the question, and that's your direct object.

For example:

> I wrote a book.   Question: "I wrote *what?*" Answer: **"a book"**

> Abraham loved children.   Question: "Abraham loved *whom?*" Answer: **"children"**

> We heard a voice.   Question: "We heard *what?*" Answer: **"a voice"**

The Direct Object In Hebrew

We wrote the three sentences in Hebrew this time. See if you can locate the **direct object**.

כָּתַבְתִּי סֵפֶר.

אַבְרָהָם אָהַב בָּנִים.

שָׁמַעְנוּ קוֹל.

We hope you found it very easy to pick out the direct object in these examples. That's all there is to it!

A Direct Object Can Be Definite Or Indefinite

The direct object of a sentence might be **definite** or **indefinite**. The three examples on the previous page all happen to be *indefinite*. Let's see what they would look like if their direct object suddenly became *definite*. We'll compare the two situations here:

Examples of <u>indefinite</u> direct objects:	**Examples of <u>definite</u> direct objects:**
I wrote <u>a book</u>.	I wrote <u>the book</u>.
Abraham loved <u>children</u>.	Abraham loved <u>the children</u>.
We heard <u>a voice</u>.	We heard <u>the voice</u>.

In English, there is no big difference between the two sentences other than to use the word "the" to indicate that the direct object is *definite*. However, in Hebrew, whenever a direct object is *definite*, we are required to add the special word אֶת as a *direct object marker*. There is not really a translation for אֶת in English. It's simply a "heads up," intended to warn us, "Hey, everybody! The direct object of this sentence is definite!" Why this became necessary in the Hebrew language is beyond all human understanding, but the word אֶת is here to stay, so you'll just have to get used to it. The good news is, after you have read it in scripture a thousand times, it will feel so natural that you'll hardly even notice it.

How To Use The Word אֶת

It boils down to one simple rule. Ask yourself: **Is the direct object of the sentence definite?** If yes, then use the word אֶת. If not, do not use the word אֶת. Examples:

I wrote a book.	כָּתַבְתִּי סֵפֶר.
I wrote the book.	כָּתַבְתִּי אֶת הַסֵּפֶר.
Abraham loved children.	אַבְרָהָם אָהַב בָּנִים.
Abraham loved the children.	אַבְרָהָם אָהַב אֶת הַבָּנִים.
Yeshua remembered Israel.	יֵשׁוּעַ זָכַר אֶת יִשְׂרָאֵל.

Did you notice on the previous page that the bottom example uses a proper noun, Israel? Remember that **proper nouns are always definite.**

Can you think of any other examples of definite nouns that we did not include on the previous page? How about nouns with possessive endings, such as the Hebrew words for *my house, your mother, his book?* Keep in mind that **nouns with possessive endings are always definite,** and therefore must be preceded by אֶת whenever they are the direct object of a sentence. Here are some examples:

Yeshua remembered His people. יֵשׁוּעַ זָכַר אֶת עַמּוֹ.

He guarded his gate. שָׁמַר אֶת שַׁעֲרוֹ.

Word Pairs (Construct Chains) And The Word אֶת

Do you recall from *Messiah's Alphabet Book 3* that construct chains (word pairs) can be either indefinite or definite? Lesson 4 in that book explains that, **when the second word of a pair is definite, the entire pair becomes definite.** Therefore, if a definite word pair is the direct object of a sentence, you must place the word אֶת ahead of it.

Yeshua remembered the land of Israel. יֵשׁוּעַ זָכַר אֶת אֶרֶץ יִשְׂרָאֵל.

More Than One Direct Object In A Sentence

If there are two or more definite direct objects in a sentence, no problem. Just make sure you place the word אֶת ahead of each direct object.

Yeshua remembered His people and His land. יֵשׁוּעַ זָכַר אֶת עַמּוֹ וְאֶת אַרְצוֹ.

The Varied Order Of Hebrew Sentences

A definite direct object may surprise you by appearing at the *beginning* of a Hebrew sentence sometimes!

He remembered his people. אֶת עַמּוֹ זָכַר.

He guarded his gate. אֶת שַׁעֲרוֹ שָׁמַר.

Exercise 2.1 - Translation Practice

Translate each sentence into English. Notice the instances in which the word אֶת is needed.

① יֵשׁוּעַ נָתַן לָהֶם לֶחֶם.

② יֵשׁוּעַ נָתַן לָהֶם אֶת הַלֶּחֶם.

③ אֶת הַלֶּחֶם נָתַן לָהֶם.

④ כָּתַבְתִּי אֶת הַסֵּפֶר.

⑤ מֹשֶׁה כָּתַב סֵפֶר טוֹב.

⑥ יֵשׁוּעַ אָהַב אֶת הָעֶבֶד הַטּוֹב.

⑦ זָכַרְתָּ אֶת שְׁמִי.

⑧ אַבְרָהָם שָׁמַע אֶת קוֹל שָׂרָה.

⑨ שָׁמַרְנוּ שַׁעַר.

⑩ שָׁמַרְנוּ אֶת שַׁעֲרוֹ.

Answers 2.1 - Translation Practice

1. Yeshua gave them bread.*
2. Yeshua gave them the bread.
3. He gave them the bread.
4. I wrote the book.
5. Moses wrote a good book.
6. Yeshua loved the good servant.
7. You remembered my name.
8. Abraham heard the voice of Sarah.
9. We guarded a gate.
10. We guarded his gate.

*Or, "Yeshua gave bread to them." As with all our exercises, please permit yourself some flexibility in your translations. We won't try to include *every* possible translation in our answer keys. Your translations will sometimes be a little bit different from ours; that's fine. They only need to be *accurate*. For example, in order to arrive at an accurate translation, you'll need to pay attention to certain things, like whether a Hebrew word is definite or indefinite. On the other hand, the exact word order of your translated sentences don't matter all that much; word order is usually just a matter of personal preference.

Exercise 2.2 - Let's Read Scripture!

For each of the following scriptures, please write the translation of each word in the blank provided underneath it. For any instances of the word אֶת you may write "d.o.m." (direct object marker) in the blank, since there is no way to translate this word into English. In this exercise, we include some of the new vocabulary words from the Word Lists in Lessons 1 and 2; some of these new words may be a bit disguised by possessive suffixes or prepositional prefixes (or are in construct form), so if a word seems totally unfamiliar, try to figure out what its root consonants are and compare them to those in your Word Lists or the glossary before you give up. Verify your answers by comparing them to our translations below.

① ... וַיְטַהֲרוּ אֶת הָעָם וְאֶת הַשְּׁעָרִים וְאֶת הַחוֹמָה.

the wall _____ _____ _____ _____ and they purified

Translation: "...and they purified the people and the gates and the wall."
Context: The priests and Levites ceremonially purified the people, the gates, and the wall of Jerusalem in preparation for its dedication (Nehemiah 12:30).

② אָהֵב יהוה שַׁעֲרֵי צִיּוֹן מִכֹּל מִשְׁכְּנוֹת יַעֲקֹב.

_____ the dwellings of _____ _____ _____ YHVH _____

Translation: "The Lord loves the gates of Zion more than all the dwellings of Jacob"
Literal Translation: "Loves YHVH the gates of Zion of all (from all) the tabernacles of Jacob."
Context: This psalm extols the glories of Zion and its special place in God's heart (Psalm 87:2).

③ וַיְקַנְאוּ בוֹ אֶחָיו - וְאָבִיו שָׁמַר אֶת הַדָּבָר.

_____ _____ _____ _____ his brothers him and envied

Translation: "His brothers envied him, but his father kept the saying in mind."
Literal Translation: "His brothers envied him, and his father kept/guarded the word/matter."
Context: Joseph tells his family his two dreams about how the whole family would bow down to him. This engenders even more jealousy among his brothers (Genesis 37:11).

Exercise 2.2 - Let's Read Scripture! *continued...*

④ וַיֹּאמֶר אֲלֵיהֶם אַתֶּם שְׁמַרְתֶּם אֵת כָּל אֲשֶׁר

_____ _____ _____ _____ and he said

צִוָּה אֶתְכֶם מֹשֶׁה עֶבֶד יהוה וַתִּשְׁמְעוּ בְּקֹלִי

_____ and you heard YHVH _____ _____ you commanded

לְכֹל אֲשֶׁר צִוִּיתִי אֶתְכֶם.

you I commanded _____ _____

Translation: "And he said to them, 'You have kept the whole of that which Moses, servant of the LORD, commanded you, and you heard my voice, to all that I have commanded you.'"

Note: The thirteenth Hebrew word of this verse is indeed a form of the verb שׁ.מ.ע *hear*, and is interpreted here as being in the *past tense*. However, this is not the particular past tense form we taught you at the beginning of this lesson, so we translated this word for you, knowing it was unfamiliar. We will teach you this alternate way of expressing past tense later in this book.

Context: Joshua commends the Reubenites, the Gadites and the half-tribe of Manasseh for their obedience and faithfulness (Joshua 22:2).

⑤ ... הַקֹּל קוֹל יַעֲקֹב וְהַיָּדִים יְדֵי עֵשָׂו.

_____ _____ _____ _____ Esau

Translation: "...the voice is the voice of Jacob, and the hands are the hands of Esau."

Context: Jacob deceives his father by wearing goatskins over his hands and neck (Genesis 27:22).

⑥ ... כְּתֹב זֹאת זִכָּרוֹן בַּסֵּפֶר ...

_____ _____ _____ write

Translation: "...write this [for] a memorial in a book..."

Context: After Joshua's men defeated the Amalekites by the miraculous power of God, the LORD commanded Moses to write the event as a memorial in a book (Exodus 17:14).

Exercise 2.2 - Let's Read Scripture! *continued...*

⑦ וַיִּכְתָּב שָׁם עַל הָאֲבָנִים אֵת מִשְׁנֵה תּוֹרַת מֹשֶׁה

_____ _____ a copy of _____ the stones _____ there and he wrote

אֲשֶׁר כָּתַב לִפְנֵי בְּנֵי יִשְׂרָאֵל.

_____ _____ _____ _____ _____

Translation: "And he wrote there upon the stones a copy of the Torah of Moses which he had written before the sons of Israel."

Note: The first Hebrew word of this verse is a form of the verb כ.ת.ב *write*, and is interpreted here as being in the *past tense*. However, this is not the particular past tense form we taught you at the beginning of this lesson, so we translated this word for you, knowing it was unfamiliar. We will teach you this alternate way of expressing past tense later in this book.

Context: Joshua leads the people in a renewal of the covenant by building an altar on Mount Ebal, writing all the words of the Torah on stones there, and reading every word aloud in the presence of the entire assembly (Joshua 8:32).

⑧ לֹא יָמוּשׁ סֵפֶר הַתּוֹרָה הַזֶּה מִפִּיךָ...

from your mouth this _____ _____ depart _____

Translation: "This book of the law shall not depart out of your mouth..."

Context: After the death of Moses, the LORD commanded Joshua to meditate and speak continually of the Torah so that he would have good success in every endeavor (Joshua 1:8).

⑨ ... אֶת קֹלְךָ שָׁמַעְתִּי בַגָּן ...

in the garden _____ _____ _____

Translation: "...I heard your voice in the garden..."

Literal Translation: "...your voice I heard in the garden..."

Context: Adam explains to God why he was hiding from Him (Genesis 3:10).

⑩ וַיַּרְא אֱלֹהִים אֶת הָאוֹר כִּי טוֹב

and saw _____ _____ _____ _____ _____

וַיַּבְדֵּל אֱלֹהִים בֵּין הָאוֹר וּבֵין הַחֹשֶׁךְ.

the darkness _____ _____ _____ _____ and divided

Translation: "And God saw the light, that it [was] good. And God divided between the light and the darkness."
Context: God divides between light and darkness at the creation of the world (Genesis 1:4).

⑪ וַיְצַו הַמֶּלֶךְ אֶת כָּל הָעָם לֵאמֹר עֲשׂוּ פֶסַח

passover   keep   saying _____ _____ _____ commanded

לַיהוה אֱלֹהֵיכֶם כַּכָּתוּב עַל סֵפֶר הַבְּרִית הַזֶּה.

this _____ _____ _____ as it is written _____ to YHVH

Translation: "And the king commanded all the people, saying, 'Keep the passover to the Lord your God, as it is written in this book of the covenant.'"
Context: King Josiah cleansed the land from the defilement of idolatry, then read the words of the Torah out loud to the people, renewing the covenant (2 Kings 23:21).

⑫ ...וְלֹא נָתַתִּי מִמֶּנּוּ לְמֵת. שָׁמַעְתִּי בְּקוֹל יהוה

YHVH _____ _____ to the dead _____ _____

אֱלֹהָי עָשִׂיתִי כְּכֹל אֲשֶׁר צִוִּיתָנִי.

you commanded me _____ _____ _____ my God

Translation: "And I have not given of it to the dead. I have heard the voice of the Lord my God; I have done according to all that You commanded me."
Context: In the midst of restating the law for the second time to Israel, Moses tells the people to recite these words to the Lord upon setting apart their tithe (Deuteronomy 26:14).

Exercise 2.2 - Let's Read Scripture! *continued...*

⑬ ...כֹּה אָמַר יְהוה אֱלֹהֵי יִשְׂרָאֵל הַדְּבָרִים אֲשֶׁר שָׁמָעְתָּ.

_____ _____ _____ _____ _____ YHVH _____ thus

Translation: "...thus said the LORD, the God of Israel [regarding] the words which you heard."
Context: The prophetess Huldah sends a message to King Josiah to inform him that God will delay sending disaster upon His people because of Josiah's sorrowful repentance (2 Kings 22:18).

⑭ וַתֵּרֶא הָאִשָּׁה כִּי טוֹב הָעֵץ לְמַאֲכָל

for food _____ the tree _____ _____ the woman and saw

...וְכִי תַאֲוָה הוּא לָעֵינַיִם

to the eyes _____ delight _____

Translation: "And the woman saw that the tree [was] good for food and that it [was] a delight to the eyes..."
Context: Eve is tempted to eat of the fruit of the forbidden tree (Genesis 3:6).

⑮ ... וַיַּעַן כָּל הָעָם קוֹל אֶחָד וַיֹּאמְרוּ כָּל הַדְּבָרִים

_____ _____ and said _____ _____ _____ and answered

אֲשֶׁר דִּבֶּר יְהוה נַעֲשֶׂה.

we will do YHVH said _____

Translation: "...and all the people answered [with] one voice, and said, 'All the words which the LORD has said, we will do.'"
Context: Upon receiving God's commandments at Mount Sinai, Moses relays them to the people who reply that they will do all the things God commanded (Exodus 24:3).

⑯ ...מָצָא חִלְקִיָּהוּ הַכֹּהֵן אֵת סֵפֶר תּוֹרַת יְהוה בְּיַד מֹשֶׁה.

_____ _____ YHVH _____ _____ _____ the priest Hilkiah found

Translation: "...Hilkiah the priest found the book of the Torah of the LORD [given by] Moses."
Note: "By the hand of Moses" is a Hebraism for "given through Moses."
Context: While carrying out King Josiah's command to restore the temple, Hilkiah finds a scroll of the Law which had been given through Moses (2 Chronicles 34:14).

The Word אֵת With Suffixes

Now that you've had some practice learning to recognize the word אֵת in scripture, we want to show you a really flexible, creative use of this word. Just by adding some simple little suffixes to it, this word can act like a series of direct object *pronouns*!

Recall from your previous studies that **Hebrew pronouns are often expressed as suffixes, especially when they are not used as the subject of a sentence.** Pronouns at the end of prepositional phrases, as you may recall, are a good example of this phenomenon. As a review, study the sentences below. The underlined words are expressed as two separate words in English, but in Hebrew, they are expressed as a single word (a preposition with a pronominal suffix):

That book belongs <u>to me</u>.	לִי	"<u>to me</u>"
The glory is <u>upon you</u>.	עָלֶיךָ	"<u>upon you</u>"
I trust <u>in him</u>.	בּוֹ	"<u>in him</u>"

In exactly the same way, there are no separate words for Hebrew pronouns which happen to follow the direct object marker אֵת in a phrase or sentence. Just as we do with prepositions, we simply attach the pronominal suffixes directly to the word אֵת. Below is a list of suffixes which have been added to the direct object marker אֵת. The suffixes will seem familiar to you, because they are just like the ones you already learned to attach to Hebrew prepositions.

us	אוֹתָנוּ	me	אוֹתִי
you (mp)	אֶתְכֶם	you (ms)	אוֹתְךָ
you (fp)	אֶתְכֶן	you (fs)	אוֹתָךְ
them (m)	אוֹתָם	him, it	אוֹתוֹ
them (f)	אוֹתָן	her, it	אוֹתָהּ

The only strange thing is, the vowel changes to an ō sound (וֹ) in the word אֵת in most of the forms above. Since this vowel can be written with or without the actual וֹ, you'll need to be prepared to recognize some alternate spellings (such as אֹתִי, for example).

So, how might these forms appear in real sentences? In the following examples, see how we *replace* each direct object *noun* with a *pronoun*, using one of the forms of אֵת with suffixes.

We loved Yeshua.	אָהַבְנוּ אֶת יֵשׁוּעַ.
We loved Him.	אָהַבְנוּ אוֹתוֹ.
He remembered Sarah.	הוּא זָכַר אֶת שָׂרָה.
He remembered her.	הוּא זָכַר אוֹתָהּ.
You wrote the books.	כָּתַבְתָּ אֶת הַסְּפָרִים.
You wrote them.	כָּתַבְתָּ אוֹתָם.

As you can see, Hebrew grammar continues to require us to use the correct form to match the gender and number of whatever pronoun we are trying to express. For example, "the books" must be replaced by the *masculine plural form* of אֵת with a suffix, because the Hebrew word for "the books" is *masculine plural*. (Now, once this word is translated into English, it becomes the word "them," which is a genderless word in English. In Hebrew, however, words like "it" or "them" always have gender, so be careful to use the correct forms when writing or speaking Hebrew.)

What's The Difference Between "It" And "It"?

At this point, our students often interrupt the lesson with an excellent question. "Hold on just a minute," they say. "Didn't we already learn two other Hebrew words which mean *it?*" They are referring to the **subject pronouns** הוּא and הִיא which can mean *it*. But in the case of the words אוֹתוֹ and אוֹתָהּ (which can also be translated *it)*, the "it" is intended to serve as a **direct object pronoun** in the sentence. Remember: *Subjects* **are words which "do" the action in the sentence, and** *objects* **are words which "receive" the action.** In Hebrew, the rule is that two different words must be used for the two different situations. English also has the same rule, but the word "it" happens to be an exception to that rule. Compare the following examples.

Most English pronouns change forms, depending on whether they serve as a subject or an object:

He guarded **him**.	**She** guarded **her**.	**They** guarded **them**.
(he=subject; him=object)	(she=subject; her=object)	(they=subject; them=object)

Certain (exceptional) English pronouns remain the same, no matter what function they serve:

It guarded **it**.
(it=subject; it=object)

The Word כָּל With Suffixes

While we're introducing cool Hebrew words that can receive suffixes, here's another, and boy, is it useful! Do you remember the word כָּל (sometimes spelled כֹּל) which means "all" or "every"? Well, you can add the same pronominal suffixes to that word, too! Here are the most common forms you'll see in scripture:

all of it (m)   כֻּלּוֹ

all of us   כֻּלָּנוּ

all of you (mp)   כֻּלְּכֶם

all of them (m)   כֻּלָּם

Note the distinctive change in vowel sound from the usual ō to the new sound "oo." Here are some examples of כָּל with suffixes, straight from the scriptures:

"...the Lord is the maker of **them all**."
(from Proverbs 22:2)

...עֹשֵׂה כֻלָּם יְהוָה.

"**All of us** are sons of one man..."
(from Genesis 42:11)

...כֻּלָּנוּ בְּנֵי אִישׁ אֶחָד נָחְנוּ

"Behold, **all you** sons of Israel..."
(from Judges 20:7)

...הִנֵּה כֻלְּכֶם בְּנֵי יִשְׂרָאֵל

Eliminate The אֵת Middleman!

Here's one more way you can use pronominal suffixes creatively. We showed you how to add pronominal suffixes directly to the word אֵת , but – here's a brand new twist – Hebrew will allow you to erase the אֵת itself and just attach its pronominal suffix directly to the verb form! It's just like "cutting out the middleman." It's kind of weird to get used to at first, but it is super helpful to know this trick. Scripture is chock full of these verbs with "tacked on" suffixes, so you'll need to at least become aware of how this works.

Here's an example. The sentence below means, "You wrote them." We could guess that the "them" might refer to words, documents or books. Let's randomly select the idea of books just to illustrate this example. In Hebrew, the word "them" is represented by a pronominal suffix added to the direct object marker אֵת. Now, imagine the word אֵת as a **middleman** who stands between the verb and the direct object (below, this is represented by the man in the suit who is standing in the gray box). The middleman's job as direct object marker is to point to the direct object, which is "them."

direct object marker + "them" pronominal suffix

"you wrote"

If we cut out the middleman, the word אֵת disappears, but its suffix persists, just like the grin of the Cheshire Cat. Here's how it looks (temporarily), right after we eliminate the middleman:

"them" pronominal suffix

"you wrote"

Since a suffix cannot stand alone like this, we just tack the floating suffix directly onto the verb:

"You wrote them."

And there again, you see that it is possible to have a one-word Hebrew sentence. Wow! That single word expresses a complete thought and tells us much about the situation being described. The diagram below will show you how much information may be gleaned by understanding the grammar of a Hebrew verb:

The suffix tells us that the items which were written are masculine and plural.

The main portion of the verb, meaning "you wrote," has a past tense form and tells us the subject is masculine and singular.

So, what does this verb form tell us? It means "You wrote them," but we also can determine that:

(A) the action was done in the **past**,

(B) the subject ("you") is **second person, masculine** and **singular** and

(C) the items which were written ("them") are **third person, masculine** and **plural**.

A little grammar knowledge will provide a wealth of information in your Bible studies. If you are able to discern the person, gender and number of each word in a Hebrew scripture, it can instantly clear up the "mysteries" which often plague those who can only read their Bibles in an English translation. Never again will you be forced to "guess" if the author was speaking to only one person ("you") or to many ("you all"), or if this "you" was a man or a woman. The original Hebrew provides an absolute answer. (This principle also applies to the Greek language of the New Testament, of course. But that's for another workbook!)

Below are some scripture portions which illustrate the technique of "cutting out the middleman":

"...the LORD, He is God. **He made us...**" (from Psalm 100:3)

...יְהוָה הוּא אֱלֹהִים הוּא עָשָׂנוּ...

"...How **have You loved us?**..." (from Malachi 1:2)

...בַּמָּה אֲהַבְתָּנוּ? ...

"...**he did** not **make me**..." (from Isaiah 29:16)

...לֹא עָשָׂנִי...

Grammar books will call this technique of adding the pronominal suffix directly to the verb **a contraction.**

Two Useful Verbs With Endings

There are two particular verbs which are used frequently in scripture. Because of their prevalence in scripture, they are often quoted in the prayers and hymns of the Jewish faith. Many of our readers are Messianic Jews who recite these words during worship and prayer in congregational services, so we wanted to introduce these two important verbs.

Word List: Verbs

make holy, consecrate, sanctify	קָ.דָ.שׁ
command	צָ.וָ.ה

The following examples show the verb קָ.דָ.שׁ, first *without* a suffix (i.e., keeping the middleman) and then *with* a suffix (cutting out the middleman).

Yeshua sanctified us.	יֵשׁוּעַ קִדֵּשׁ אוֹתָנוּ.
Yeshua sanctified us.	יֵשׁוּעַ קִדְּשָׁנוּ.

The following examples show the verb צָ.וָ.ה in the same two situations.

Yeshua commanded us.*	יֵשׁוּעַ צִוָּה אוֹתָנוּ.
Yeshua commanded us.*	יֵשׁוּעַ צִוָּנוּ.

Grammar experts would say that the bottom two sentences of each example represent "contractions," since the middleman gets cut out, and the suffix gets grafted onto the verb itself.

---

*Please note that the verb צָ.וָ.ה has an exceptional spelling – a dot in the letter *vav* which makes it look like a vowel (*shoo-rook*). However, it is not pronounced as a vowel in these words. In these verb forms, we ignore the dot and pronounce this *vav* like "v" as in "vase." Therefore, the correct pronunciation of the two forms above is *tsih-VAH* and *tsih-VAH-noo*.

Exercise 2.3 - Let's Read Scripture!

For each of the following scriptures, please write the translation of each word in the blank provided underneath it. For this exercise, we found some scriptures which contain אֵת with suffixes, כָּל with suffixes, and certain verbs with suffixes. These suffixes will be *pronominal object* suffixes, having the meanings of *him, her, them, us,* etc., as demonstrated earlier in the lesson. For any instance of the word אֵת which does *not* have a suffix, you should simply write "d.o.m." (direct object marker) in its blank.

① לְכֻלָּם   נָתַן   לָאִישׁ   חֲלִפוֹת   שְׂמָלֹת...

_____   _____   to each man   changes of   garments

Translation: "To all of them he gave each man changes of clothes..."
Context: After Joseph revealed his identity to his brothers, he gave them provisions and clothes for their return journey (Genesis 45:22).

② ...וַיהוה   הִפְגִּיעַ   בּוֹ   אֵת   עֲוֹן   כֻּלָּנוּ.

and YHVH   caused to fall   _____   _____   iniquity of   _____

Translation: "...and the Lord has laid on him the iniquity of us all."
Literal Translation: "...and the Lord has made to fall in him (on him) the iniquity of us all."
Note: The word אֵת in this verse uses the less common spelling having a *tsay-ray:* אֵת
Context: This famous verse of messianic prophecy explains how God placed the punishment for our sins and guilt upon His Son so that we might be forgiven (Isaiah 53:6).

③ ...כִּי   אֲנַחְנוּ   יַחַד   נִבְנֶה   לַיהוה   אֱלֹהֵי   יִשְׂרָאֵל

_____   _____   together   we will build   to YHVH   _____   _____

כַּאֲשֶׁר   צִוָּנוּ   הַמֶּלֶךְ   כּוֹרֶשׁ   מֶלֶךְ   פָּרָס.

as   _____   _____   Cyrus   _____   Persia

Translation: "...for we together will build for the Lord the God of Israel, as the king – Cyrus king of Persia – commanded us."
Context: This was Zerubbabel's answer to the enemies of Judah, who were attempting to sabotage the rebuilding of the temple (Ezra 4:3).

---

④ וַיְבָרֶךְ אֱלֹהִים אֶת יוֹם הַשְּׁבִיעִי וַיְקַדֵּשׁ אֹתוֹ...

_____ and consecrated   the seventh   _____ ____ _____ and blessed

Translation: "And God blessed the seventh day and consecrated it..."
Context: After God created the universe, He rested on the seventh day and declared it a holy day (Genesis 2:3).

⑤ ...קְנֵה אֹתָנוּ וְאֶת אַדְמָתֵנוּ בַּלָּחֶם וְנִהְיֶה

and will be   for food   our land   _____ _____ buy

אֲנַחְנוּ וְאַדְמָתֵנוּ עֲבָדִים לְפַרְעֹה...

to Pharaoh   _____ and our land   _____

Translation: "...buy us and our land for food, and we and our land will be slaves to Pharaoh..."
Context: The famine in Egypt became so severe that everyone in Egypt sold all that they had to Pharaoh in exchange for food – including their land and their very lives (Genesis 47:19).

⑥ וַיִּבְרָא אֱלֹהִים אֶת הָאָדָם בְּצַלְמוֹ – בְּצֶלֶם אֱלֹהִים

_____ in the image of   in His image   the man   _____ _____ and created

בָּרָא אֹתוֹ, זָכָר וּנְקֵבָה בָּרָא אֹתָם.

_____ he created   and a female   a male   _____ he created

Translation: "And God created the man in His image; in the image of God He created him, a male and a female He created them."
Note: The first word in this verse means "he created" but is in a variant form of the past tense. We will teach you in future lessons all about this other way of expressing the past tense. This word means the same thing as the spelling בָּרָא which appears twice in the second half of the verse – בָּרָא will probably seem more familiar to you (it somewhat follows the basic pattern of past tense which we taught in Lesson 1).
Context: This verse describes God's creation of human beings (Gen. 1:27).

Exercise 2.3 - Let's Read Scripture! *continued...*

⑦ וַיֹּאמֶר פַּרְעֹה אֶל יוֹסֵף, רְאֵה, נָתַתִּי אֹתְךָ

_____ _____ See, Joseph, _____ Pharaoh and said

עַל כָּל אֶרֶץ מִצְרָיִם.

_____ _____ _____

Translation: "And Pharaoh said to Joseph, 'See, I have set you over all the land of Egypt.'"

Literal Translation: "And Pharaoh said to Joseph, 'See, I have given you over all the land of Egypt.'"

Context: After Joseph interprets Pharaoh's dreams about the coming years of famine and urges Pharaoh to prepare for it by storing large amounts of food, Pharaoh puts him in charge of the storage program and the entire land of Egypt (Genesis 41:41).

⑧ אָהַבְתִּי אֶתְכֶם, אָמַר יהוה. וַאֲמַרְתֶּם, בַּמָּה אֲהַבְתָּנוּ?

_____ in what _____ YHVH _____ _____ _____

Translation: " 'I have loved you,' said the LORD. And you said, 'In what have You loved us?'"

Context: The prophet Malachi opens his book with these words of the LORD, which expose the people's innermost feelings of ingratitude and doubt (Malachi 1:2).

⑨ דְּעוּ כִּי יהוה הוּא אֱלֹהִים – הוּא עָשָׂנוּ...

_____ _____ _____ _____ YHVH _____ know

Translation: "Know that the LORD, He is God – He has made us..."

Context: These words are from a Psalm urging the people to joyfully proclaim praises to God. The New Living Translation has the full verse as, "Acknowledge that the LORD is God! He made us, and we are his. We are his people, the sheep of his pasture." (Psalm 100:3).

⑩ וְהֵבֵאתִי אֶתְכֶם אֶל הָאָרֶץ אֲשֶׁר נָשָׂאתִי אֶת יָדִי

_____ _____ I lifted _____ _____ _____ _____ and I will bring

לָתֵת אֹתָהּ לְאַבְרָהָם, לְיִצְחָק, וּלְיַעֲקֹב, וְנָתַתִּי אֹתָהּ

_____ _____ * _____ _____ _____ _____ to give

לָכֶם מוֹרָשָׁה – אֲנִי יהוה.

YHVH _____ for a possession _____

Translation: "and I will bring you to the land which I have lifted up My hand (swore) to give it to Abraham, to Isaac, and to Jacob, and I have given it to you, a possession. I am the Lᴏʀᴅ."

*Note: The verb form of the fourteenth Hebrew word in this verse, וְנָתַתִּי , can either be translated "and I have given" (which is the past tense form you learned in Lesson 1) or "I will give" (future tense). There is a special use of the letter *vav* as a prefix which can alter the tense of this verb. We will teach you this technique later in this book. Both translations are technically correct; both can be simultaneously true. Indeed, God *had already* given the promised land to these, Abraham's descendants, in a formal covenant He had made with Abraham (and with all of Abraham's descendants to come). However, it is also true that He would, in the future, *give* this land to the sons of Israel as their own possession, *after* their exodus from Egypt, and *after* their successful entry into the promised land. Hebrew scripture is full of such multiple renderings of verb tenses, so translators must keep an open mind to all possible meanings.

Context: The Lᴏʀᴅ tells Moses to inform the people that He will soon bring them out from under their slavery to the Egyptians and that they will then go on to possess His gift – the promised land of Canaan (Exodus 6:8).

Exercise 2.4 - Lesson Recap

Mark each statement below with a **"T"** for "True" or an **"F"** for "False" in the small blank to its left. If the statement is false, write the reason why it is false in the long blank below the statement, or provide a few examples demonstrating why it is false (i.e., "counterexamples").

_____ 1. The word אֶת, in some form, must *always* precede a direct object.

_____

_____ 2. The word אֵת (spelled as shown here), has no translation in English.

_____

_____ 3. Hebrew subject pronouns have different forms (spellings) than object pronouns.

_____

_____ 4. Pronominal suffixes may be attached to the word אֶת.

_____

_____ 5. The word אֵת with a pronominal suffix has no translation in English.

_____

_____ 6. It is not possible to attach a pronominal suffix to the word כָּל.

_____

_____ 7. It is possible to attach a pronominal suffix directly to a verb.

_____

_____ 8. If the word אֵת would ordinarily be required but has been removed, it's because its pronominal suffix has been attached directly to the verb.

_____

_____ 9. The person, gender and number of a suffix added to the word אֵת are unimportant.

_____

_____ 10. The person, gender and number of a suffix added to *any* word are important.

_____

Answers 2.4 - Lesson Recap

1. F   The word אֵת is only required to precede a *definite* direct object.
2. T
3. T
4. T
5. F   The word אֵת with suffixes is translated into object pronouns such as *him, us, me, it*, etc.
6. F   You can attach pronominal suffixes to כָּל. A few examples: כֻּלָּם or כֻּלָּנוּ.
7. T
8. T
9. F   These attributes are *essential* for translating אֵת with a suffix into the correct object pronoun.
10. T

סֵפֶר	קוֹל
שַׁעַר	אֵת, אֶת
כִּי	אֲשֶׁר, שֶׁ־
כ.ת.ב	שׁ.מ.ע
ק.ד.שׁ	צ.ו.ה

SAY-fehr
book, scroll

noun, masculine, singular

(This word was introduced in Book 4, Lesson 2)

kōhl
voice, sound

noun, masculine, singular

(This word was introduced in Book 4, Lesson 2)

shah-AR
gate

noun, masculine, singular

(This word was introduced in Book 4, Lesson 2)

eht, ayt
direct object marker

(This word was introduced in Book 4, Lesson 2)

kee
because, that

conjunction (or other part of speech)

(This word was introduced in Book 4, Lesson 2)

ah-SHEHR, sheh-
which, who, that

pronoun (beginning a descriptive clause)

(This word was introduced in Book 4, Lesson 2)

write

verb

(This word was introduced in Book 4, Lesson 2)

hear, heed

verb

(This word was introduced in Book 4, Lesson 2)

make holy, consecrate

verb

(This word was introduced in Book 4, Lesson 2)

command

verb

(This word was introduced in Book 4, Lesson 2)

Lesson 3:
The Verb "To Be" And More

Early in your studies, way back in Book 1, you learned that an entire sentence could be written using only nouns, which we called a "noun sentence." We had a cartoon of Tarzan trying to read a Hebrew noun sentence in its literal order as he swung on a vine, gleefully shouting, "You father!" Jane patiently tried to correct him, inserting a form of the verb *to be*: "You *are* a father."

Pretty quickly, you mastered this skill of inserting the verb *to be* as needed. However, all the noun sentences you have translated in this manner have always been in the **present tense.** We gave you a simple Hebrew noun sentence to translate, and you then inserted the word *am, is,* or *are*. It may surprise you to learn that there actually is a Hebrew verb *to be* which has special forms for the **past tense,** i.e., *was* and *were*. This lesson will teach you these irregular past tense forms.

Before we begin, we have more great Biblical vocabulary to share. These words will really open up the scriptures to you! Get ready for some powerful new knowledge.

Word List: Masculine Nouns

			time, season*	z'-*MAHN* ms	זְמַן
deeds, acts *mah-ah-SEEM* mp	מַעֲשִׂים	deed, act*	*mah-ah-SEH** ms		מַעֲשֶׂה
		will, favor, acceptance	*rah-TSŌN* ms		רָצוֹן

*Important notes about the words above:

The plural form of the word *time/season* זְמַן occurs so infrequently in scripture and Jewish liturgy that its spelling is rarely taught in textbooks. This word for time/season sometimes has spiritual overtones connoting a "special time" remembering acts of God's supernatural deliverance and/or His holy days.

Notice the root letters of the noun *deed/act* מַעֲשֶׂה which come from a verb you know: ע.שׂ.ה *make, do.*

lands	ah-dah-MŌT	fp	אֲדָמוֹת	ground, land*	ah-dah-MAH	fs	אֲדָמָה
				redemption	g'-oo-LAH	fs	גְּאֻלָּה
commandments	mits-VŌT*	fp	מִצְוֹת	commandment	mits-VAH	fs	מִצְוָה
families	mish-pah-CHŌT	fp	מִשְׁפָּחוֹת	family	mish-pah-CHAH	fs	מִשְׁפָּחָה
souls	n'-fah-SHŌT	fp	נְפָשׁוֹת	soul	NEH-fesh	fs	נֶפֶשׁ
cities*	ah-REEM	fp	עָרִים	city	eer	fs	עִיר
prayers	t'-fih-LŌT	fp	תְּפִלּוֹת	prayer	t'-fih-LAH	fs	תְּפִלָּה

*Important notes about the words above:

The word *ground, land* אֲדָמָה can mean the same thing as a word you already know: אֶרֶץ. Although these two words have overlapping meaning and can act as synonyms, they have slightly different senses insofar as how frequently they hold different connotations in scripture. For example, אֶרֶץ refers to *a specific nation's land or territory* in over 70% of its occurrences in scripture; the remaining 30% or so have the global, generic meanings of *homeland, property, soil,* or *earth.* On the other hand, the word אֲדָמָה refers to the global meanings of *earth, soil, produce, dust, arable ground* or *land* in over 80% of its scriptural occurrences; the remaining 20% or so refer to a *specific nation's land* or an *individual's property.* The root letters of the term אֲדָמָה provides a glimpse into one of its meanings. Our English word *Adam* is, in Hebrew, אָדָם (i.e., *humankind*) and has the same root letters as אֲדָמָה. Genesis 2:7 places these words in close relationship to each other: "And the LORD God formed the *man (adam)* אָדָם from the dust of the *ground (adamah)* אֲדָמָה..."

The plural form of the noun *commandments* מִצְוֹת pronounces the "v" sound of the letter *vav* as well as the *cholam's* "oh" sound: *mits-VŌHT.* This Hebrew noun comes from the same roots as the verb you learned in the last lesson: צ.ו.ה *command.*

The plural form of the noun *cities* עָרִים is an exception in that it takes a *masculine plural* suffix. It remains a feminine plural noun, however.

A Noun With Common Gender

ways, roads   *d'rah-CHEEM* cp   דְּרָכִים   way, road   *DEH-rech*   cs   דֶּרֶךְ

Well, here's a new one for you. **There are certain Hebrew nouns which can have either masculine or feminine gender,** and this is defined as **"common gender."** The word *way, road* דֶּרֶךְ is one such example. Since it appears more frequently in *masculine* gender in scripture, certain dictionaries (especially Bible dictionaries) choose to list its lexical form under the heading of "masculine." In reality, it can make an appearance in *either* gender, depending on the situation. Deuteronomy 17:16 (" ...בַּדֶּרֶךְ הַזֶּה... ") is an example in which it is *masculine*. Exodus 18:20 (" ...הַדֶּרֶךְ יֵלְכוּ בָהּ... ") is an example in which it is *feminine*. One way you can tell which gender this noun is assuming is by examining the gender of the other words modifying it. Note: Even though this word is a common gender noun, its plural form takes the *masculine* suffix.

Word List: Verbs

redeem	ג.א.ל
be, exist, become	ה.י.ה
sit, dwell	י.שׁ.ב

Note that the verb *redeem* ג.א.ל has the same root letters as the noun *redemption* גְּאֻלָּה from the Word List on the previous page. Recognizing root letters can be a powerful tool to help you memorize lots of new vocabulary very quickly!

in the beginning*	*b'-ray-SHEET*	בְּרֵאשִׁית
always, continually	*tah-MEED*	תָּמִיד

*Important notes about the words above:

In the beginning בְּרֵאשִׁית is a very important Hebrew word encompassing vast meaning, and holds the honor of being the first word of the Hebrew Bible (Genesis 1:1). Jewish tradition and liturgy often use this word as a synonym for *God's creation of the entire universe.* A vast subject, indeed.

Word List: *This, These, That* and *Those*... As Adjectives

that	*hah-HOO*	ms	הַהוּא		this	*hah-ZEH*	ms	הַזֶּה
that	*hah-HEE*	fs	הַהִיא		this	*hah-ZŌT*	fs	הַזֹּאת
those	*hah-HAYM*	mp*	הָהֵם		these	*hah-AY-leh*	cp	הָאֵלֶּה

*Important notes about the words above:

You have already learned all of these words, except you did *not* learn them with the definite article prefix הַ. If you try to translate these words literally, you end up with "the this" or "the those," which, frankly, sounds ridiculous. They are not actually translated this way. The reason for attaching the definite article prefix in these particular spellings is to allow the words to be used **as adjectives to modify definite nouns.** We will explore this concept in detail in the next pages, and you'll get plenty of examples for clarification.

You may have noticed that the word *those* הָהֵם is in *masculine* form and thus would modify a *masculine plural* noun. "Isn't there a feminine form of this word?" you may be asking. The answer is, yes, there is a word *those* הָהֵנָּה which is used as an adjective to modify *feminine plural* nouns, but it only appears one time in the entire Bible! We did not wish to burden you with memorizing this rare form, so we left it off the list. (On the other hand, the masculine form הָהֵם in this particular spelling appears more than 40 times in scripture. It also appears in a variety of other spellings over 800 times in scripture – so it is necessary to know this word!)

This And *These,* Used In Different Ways

In English, the words *this* and *these* can be used in many different ways. We'll look at two of those ways right now. The first way is to place them at the beginning of a sentence, where they act like a pronoun. The second way is to place them right next to a noun elsewhere in the sentence, where they act like an adjective (because they describe the noun). Below are examples of the two ways, side by side.

<u>Like a pronoun:</u>

This is the man.

This is the prayer.

These are the books.

These are the daughters.

<u>Like an adjective:</u>

this man

this prayer

these books

these daughters

In Hebrew, the two ways of using these words dictates both where they will appear in the sentence and whether they will have the prefix ה. Let's use the same example sentences above, but this time, we'll also translate them into Hebrew. See if you can catch the pattern.

<u>Like a pronoun:</u>

This is the man.   זֶה הָאִישׁ.

This is the prayer.   זֹאת הַתְּפִלָּה.

These are the books.   אֵלֶּה הַסְּפָרִים.

These are the daughters.   אֵלֶּה הַבָּנוֹת.

<u>Like an adjective:</u>

this man   הָאִישׁ הַזֶּה

this prayer   הַתְּפִלָּה הַזֹּאת

these books   הַסְּפָרִים הָאֵלֶּה

these daughters   הַבָּנוֹת הָאֵלֶּה

The first situation (on the left side) is one which should feel familiar to you. This is the same manner in which you have already been taught to use these words: Use them to begin the sentence, and use them *without* the ה prefix. But on the right side, the prefix ה has been added, because the word is acting like an **adjective**, modifying a definite noun. Remember the rule that Hebrew adjectives require the addition of the prefix ה whenever they follow a definite noun. This is just another case of that rule.

Here are some examples from scripture using הַזֶּה, הַזֹּאת, and הָאֵלֶּה.

"...the glory of **this** house..."
(from Haggai 2:9)

...כְּבוֹד הַבַּיִת הַזֶּה...

"...I have given **this** land."
(from Genesis 15:18)

...נָתַתִּי אֶת הָאָרֶץ הַזֹּאת.

"...I have done all **these** things."
(from 1 Kings 18:36)

...עָשִׂיתִי אֶת כָּל הַדְּבָרִים הָאֵלֶּה.

That And *Those*, Used As Adjectives

The words הַהוּא and הַהִיא are translated *that*, and the word הָהֵם is translated *those*. Again, these words are used to modify a definite noun. Let's look at some examples from the scriptures which include these three words.

"...in **that** day the king gave..."
(from Esther 8:1)

...בַּיּוֹם הַהוּא נָתַן הַמֶּלֶךְ

"...upon **that** land..."
(from Jeremiah 25:13)

...עַל הָאָרֶץ הַהִיא

"In **those** days there was no king in Israel..."
(from Judges 17:6)

...בַּיָּמִים הָהֵם אֵין מֶלֶךְ בְּיִשְׂרָאֵל

Past Tense Of The Verb "Be" – ה.י.ה

Now that we've explained all the new vocabulary for this lesson, it's finally time to teach you the past tense forms of the verb "be" in Hebrew.

ה.י.ה *be*

הָיִינוּ	*1cp* we were	הָיִיתִי	*1cs* I was
הֱיִיתֶם	*2mp* you were	הָיִיתָ	*2ms* you were
הֱיִיתֶן	*2fp* you were	הָיִית	*2fs* you were
הָיוּ	*3mp* they were	הָיָה	*3ms* he/it was
הָיוּ	*3fp* they were	הָיְתָה	*3fs* she/it was

The forms used the *least* in scripture are 1cs, 2ms, 2fs, and 3fp. If you have limited time, it's best to spend more time memorizing the other forms in the list. Remember, these are *past tense* forms. If you need to express the verb "be" in the *present tense*, a simple noun sentence will do.

Examples Using The Past Tense Of The Verb "Be" (ה.י.ה)

Below are some pairs of examples which show a **present tense** noun sentence followed by the same sentence rewritten in the **past tense** using the verb ה.י.ה.

I am a good son.	אֲנִי בֵּן טוֹב.
I was a good son.	אֲנִי הָיִיתִי בֵּן טוֹב.

Abraham is in the city.	אַבְרָהָם בָּעִיר.
Abraham was in the city.	אַבְרָהָם הָיָה בָּעִיר.

You are slaves.	אַתֶּם עֲבָדִים.
You were slaves.	הֱיִיתֶם עֲבָדִים.

As with other verbs, each the ten forms of past tense ה.י.ה. **expresses the subject pronoun as well as the verb itself**. You have the option of explicitly expressing that pronoun in Hebrew (as in the first example pair above), or not (as in the last example pair).

Just like other verbs, **the meaning of this verb in the past tense is flexible**. For example, the 3ms form might simply mean *he was*, but could also be translated *he had become, he became, he had been, he existed*, etc. Translators use a variety of English words to express this verb's meaning.

How about some scriptural examples showing ה.י.ה. in action? Here are some good ones:

"...I **was** king over Israel..." (from Ecclesiastes 1:12)	...הָיִיתִי מֶלֶךְ עַל יִשְׂרָאֵל...
"...the man **has become** like one of Us..." (from Genesis 3:22)	...הָאָדָם הָיָה כְּאַחַד מִמֶּנּוּ...
"...we **were** slaves to Pharaoh in Egypt..." (from Deuteronomy 6:21)	...עֲבָדִים הָיִינוּ לְפַרְעֹה בְּמִצְרָיִם...

Using The Verb ה.י.ה To Say "Had"

You probably remember from Book 3 about those prepositions which are prefixes. One of those prepositional prefixes, לְ, can be used to show *possession*. Literally, this preposition means *to* or *for*. However, you may translate it in such a way that it indicates ownership. To refresh your memory, here are some examples:

To David is a house.   לְדָוִד בַּיִת.

To us there are blessings.   לָנוּ בְּרָכוֹת.

Note that the above Hebrew sentences don't have any verbs in them; they are basic noun sentences. Looking at our English translations, you'll see we needed to insert the verb *be* ("is," "are"). Those translated sentences, while technically correct, sound a bit awkward. Let's translate them again, but this time we'll change them to something that sounds more natural in English.

David has a house.   לְדָוִד בַּיִת.

We have blessings.   לָנוּ בְּרָכוֹת.

Ahhh... that's better. Here, we captured the essence of the meaning in a way that "flows smoothly" in English. Nice translation. However, it's important to remember that the original Hebrew didn't use *any* verbs in these sentences showing possession. *We're* the ones who artificially imposed the verbs "has" and "have" on these sentences... and the only reason we chose these particular verbs was because they better suited our English *syntax* (way of arranging words).

Here's a question. Can we somehow express ownership in the *past tense* in Hebrew? For example, is there any way we could say, "David *had* a house"? Well, yes, we can. To do this, though, we need to go all the way back to our method of inserting the verb *be* and understand that the verb *be* has <u>always</u> existed within Hebrew noun sentences (although it has been unspoken and unwritten up until now, because the examples we have taught you have always been in the present tense). This time, watch as the Hebrew language actually uses the verb *be*, ה.י.ה, but inserts its *past tense* forms.

To David was a house.   לְדָוִד הָיָה בַּיִת.

To us were blessings.   לָנוּ הָיוּ בְּרָכוֹת.

Rewriting our translations to something a little less awkward, we finally end up with:

David had a house.   לְדָוִד הָיָה בַּיִת.

We had blessings.   לָנוּ הָיוּ בְּרָכוֹת.

Easy, right? Right!

How To Say "Not Have"

If you want to say "not have" in the *present* tense, just add the word אֵין to a noun sentence as follows:

There is not to David a house.
or David does not have a house.

אֵין לְדָוִד בַּיִת.

There are not to us blessings.
or We do not have blessings.

אֵין לָנוּ בְּרָכוֹת.

If you want to say "not have" in the *past* tense, use the word לֹא as follows:

There was not to David a house.
or David did not have a house.

לֹא הָיָה לְדָוִד בַּיִת.

There were not to us blessings.
or We did not have blessings.

לֹא הָיוּ לָנוּ בְּרָכוֹת.

Aside from learning to talk like Yoda, it's fairly simple to say "have" and "not have" in Hebrew. You're ready for the exercises at the end of the lesson! Here we go!

> sigh <

Why is not to us ice cream any more? Hmmm? *All* of it did Luke eat last night? Hmmm?

Rooming with Yoda could be annoying from time to time.

Exercise 3.1 - Riddle Review

Match each phrase or sentence to its translation, then write its circled "code letter" in the space provided. The circled letters will spell the answer to the riddle.

Where is baseball mentioned in the Bible?

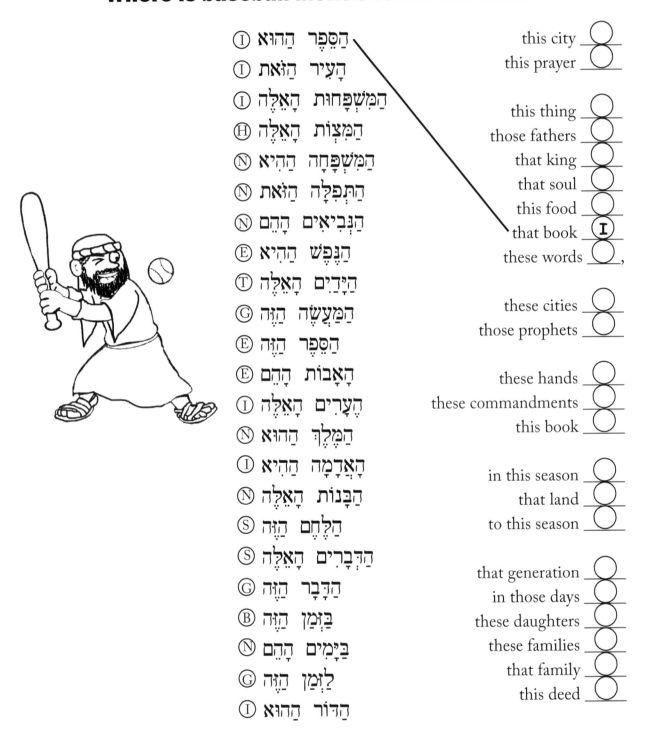

Ⓘ הַסֵּפֶר הַהוּא — this city ◯
Ⓘ הָעִיר הַזֹּאת — this prayer ◯

Ⓘ הַמִּשְׁפָּחוֹת הָאֵלֶּה — this thing ◯
Ⓗ הַמִּצְוֹת הָאֵלֶּה — those fathers ◯
Ⓝ הַמִּשְׁפָּחָה הַהִיא — that king ◯
Ⓝ הַתְּפִלָּה הַזֹּאת — that soul ◯
Ⓝ הַנְּבִיאִים הָהֵם — this food ◯
Ⓔ הַנֶּפֶשׁ הַהִיא — that book Ⓘ
Ⓣ הַיָּדִים הָאֵלֶּה — these words ◯,

Ⓖ הַמַּעֲשֶׂה הַזֶּה — these cities ◯
Ⓔ הַסֵּפֶר הַזֶּה — those prophets ◯

Ⓔ הָאָבוֹת הָהֵם — these hands ◯
Ⓘ הֶעָרִים הָאֵלֶּה — these commandments ◯
Ⓝ הַמֶּלֶךְ הַהוּא — this book ◯

Ⓘ הָאֲדָמָה הַהִיא — in this season ◯
Ⓝ הַבָּנוֹת הָאֵלֶּה — that land ◯
Ⓢ הַלֶּחֶם הַזֶּה — to this season ◯

Ⓢ הַדְּבָרִים הָאֵלֶּה — that generation ◯
Ⓖ הַדָּבָר הַזֶּה — in those days ◯
Ⓑ בַּזְּמַן הַזֶּה — these daughters ◯
Ⓝ בַּיָּמִים הָהֵם — these families ◯
Ⓖ לַזְּמַן הַזֶּה — that family ◯
Ⓘ הַדּוֹר הַהוּא — this deed ◯

Answer: In Genesis, in the big inning.

Exercise 3.2 - Crossword Review

Write the English translation for each Hebrew word below.

Across

2. דֶּרֶךְ

7. אֲדָמָה

8. תָּמִיד

10. מִשְׁפָּחָה

11. מַעֲשֶׂה

12. בְּרֵאשִׁית

Down

1. מִצְוָה

3. רָצוֹן

4. עִיר

5. נֶפֶשׁ

6. תְּפִלָּה

9. זְמַן

Answers 3.2 - Crossword Review

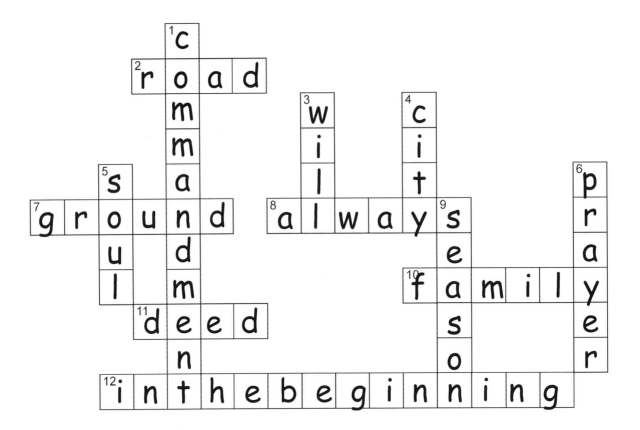

Across

2. דֶּרֶךְ
7. אֲדָמָה
8. תָּמִיד
10. מִשְׁפָּחָה
11. מַעֲשֶׂה
12. בְּרֵאשִׁית

Down

1. מִצְוָה
3. רָצוֹן
4. עִיר
5. נֶפֶשׁ
6. תְּפִלָּה
9. זְמַן

Exercise 3.3 - Translation Practice

Translate the following Hebrew sentences. Make sure to read each Hebrew sentence out loud.

① הָיִינוּ בְּבֵית הַתְּפִלָּה בְּיוֹם הַזִּכָּרוֹן.

_____

② יֵשׁוּעַ גָּאַל אֶת הָאֲנָשִׁים הָאֵלֶּה מִידֵי הָרְשָׁעִים.

_____

③ לִבְנֵי יִשְׂרָאֵל הָיוּ מִצְוֹת קְדוֹשׁוֹת.

_____

④ הָאָב וְהַבֵּן שָׁמְעוּ אֶת הַתְּפִלָּה אֲשֶׁר אָמַר עַבְדָּם.

_____

⑤ זֶה הַנָּבִיא שֶׁאָמַר אֶת הַדְּבָרִים הָאֵלֶּה עַל גְּאֻלַּת הָעוֹלָם.

_____

⑥ הָעֶבֶד הַטּוֹב שָׁמַר אֶת שַׁעֲרֵי עִירוֹ תָּמִיד.

_____

⑦ הַדֶּרֶךְ אֶל גְּאֻלָּה הָיָה תָּמִיד דֶּרֶךְ תְּפִלָּה.

_____

Answers 3.3 - Translation Practice

① We were in the house of prayer on the day of the memorial. (_or_ day of remembrance)*

② Yeshua redeemed these men from the hands of the wicked ones.

③ The children of Israel had holy commandments.

④ The father and the son heard the prayer which their servant said.

⑤ This is the prophet who said these things about the redemption of the world.

⑥ The good servant guarded the gates of his city continually.

⑦ The way to redemption has always been a way of prayer.

*Only one of many possible translations is provided for each answer here. Please note that there are many different ways to accurately translate all of these sentences into English.

Exercise 3.4 - Let's Read Scripture!

For each of the following scriptures, please write the translation of each word in the blank provided underneath it. Remember that nouns can change their endings when they appear in construct form (word pairs), so if you don't recognize a word at first, compare its root letters to those in the Word Lists or the glossary before you give up.

① בְּרֵאשִׁית בָּרָא אֱלֹהִים אֵת הַשָּׁמַיִם וְאֵת הָאָרֶץ.

_____ _____ _____ _____ created _____

Translation: "In the beginning, God created the heavens and the earth."
Context: The first verse of the Bible which begins the account of creation (Genesis 1:1).

② אֲשֶׁר הָיָה דְבַר יהוה אֶל יִרְמְיָהוּ הַנָּבִיא אֶל עֵילָם

Elam _____ Jeremiah _____ YHVH _____ _____

בְּרֵאשִׁית מַלְכוּת צִדְקִיָּה מֶלֶךְ יְהוּדָה...

Judah _____ Zedekiah _____ _____

Translation: "This was the word of the LORD to Jeremiah the prophet concerning Elam, at the start of the reign of Zedekiah, king of Judah..."
Literal Translation: "That which was the word of YHVH to Jeremiah the prophet to Elam in the beginning of the kingdom of Zedekiah king of Judah..."
Context: God brings a prophecy against the country of Elam (Jeremiah 49:34).

③ וְאֵד יַעֲלֶה מִן הָאָרֶץ וְהִשְׁקָה אֶת כָּל פְּנֵי הָאֲדָמָה.

_____ _____ _____ and watered _____ _____ went up and a mist

Translation: "A mist came up from the earth and watered all the surface (face) of the ground."
Context: This was the method by which God brought water into the soil before there was ever any rain (Genesis 2:6).

Exercise 3.4 - Let's Read Scripture! continued...

④ לַכֹּל זְמָן וְעֵת לְכָל חֵפֶץ תַּחַת הַשָּׁמָיִם.

_____ under   purpose   _____ and a time _____ _____

Translation: "For everything [there is] a season and a time for every purpose under heaven."
Context: The first verse and theme statement of chapter three of Ecclesiastes (Ecclesiates 3:1).

⑤ וַיֹּאמֶר לָהֶם יוֹסֵף, מָה הַמַּעֲשֶׂה הַזֶּה אֲשֶׁר עֲשִׂיתֶם?

_____ _____ _____ _____ _____ Joseph _____ and said

Translation: "And Joseph said to them, 'What [is] this deed which you have done?'"
Context: Joseph accuses his brothers of stealing his silver cup after ordering his steward to plant it in the youngest one's bag (Genesis 44:15a).

⑥ רְצוֹן מֶלֶךְ לְעֶבֶד מַשְׂכִּיל...

wise _____ _____ _____

Translation: "A king's favor [is] toward a wise servant..."
Literal Translation: "Favor of a king [is] for a wise servant..."
Context: A proverb in a chapter contrasting wisdom against foolishness (Proverbs 14:35).

⑦ וְזֹאת לְפָנִים בְּיִשְׂרָאֵל עַל הַגְּאוּלָה...

_____ _____ formerly _____

Translation: "And this [was the custom] in former times in Israel concerning redemption..."
Literal Translation: "And this formerly in Israel about the redemption..."
Context: The old-fashioned custom of sealing all legal transfers in Israel by removing one's sandal (including redemption of land or bride by a close kinsman) is described here (Ruth 4:7).

Exercise 3.4 - Let's Read Scripture! *continued...*

(8) ...גָּאַל יהוה עַבְדּוֹ יַעֲקֹב.

_____ _____ YHVH _____

Translation: "...The Lord has redeemed His servant Jacob."
Context: The prophet Isaiah speaks about God's redemption of a remnant of His people, which follows after a time of chastisement because of their idolatry (Isaiah 48:20).

(9) וּשְׁלֹמֹה יָשַׁב עַל כִּסֵּא דָוִד אָבִיו...

_____ _____ the throne of _____ _____ and Solomon

Translation: "And Solomon sat upon the throne of David his father..."
Context: The account of the death of David and Solomon's ascension to his father's throne (1 Kings 2:12).

(10) אַבְרָם יָשַׁב בְּאֶרֶץ כְּנַעַן וְלוֹט יָשַׁב בְּעָרֵי הַכִּכָּר...

the plain _____ _____ and Lot Canaan _____ _____ Abram

Translation: "Abram dwelled in the land of Canaan, and Lot dwelled in the cities of the plain..."
Context: Abram and Lot part ways, and Lot decides to pitch his tents near Sodom (Genesis 13:12)

(11) ...לַעֲשׂוֹת אֶת הַמִּצְוָה וְאֶת הַתּוֹרָה אֲשֶׁר

_____ _____ _____ _____ to do

צִוָּה אֶתְכֶם מֹשֶׁה עֶבֶד יהוה.

YHVH _____ _____

Translation: "...to observe the commandment and the law which Moses the servant of the Lord commanded you."
Context: Joshua sends off the Reubenites, the Gadites and the half-tribe of Manasseh with a blessing along with this reminder to carefully observe everything God commanded them (Joshua 22:5).

Exercise 3.4 - Let's Read Scripture! *continued...*

⑫ ...מִי אָנֹכִי? וּמִי חַיַּי, מִשְׁפַּחַת אָבִי בְּיִשְׂרָאֵל,

_____ _____ _____ my life _____ _____ _____

כִּי אֶהְיֶה חָתָן לַמֶּלֶךְ?

_____ son-in-law I should be _____

Translation: "Who am I, and what is my life [or] my father's family in Israel, that I should become the king's son-in-law?"

Literal Translation: "Who am I? And who is my life, the family of my father in Israel, that I should become son-in-law to the king?"

Context: David refuses King Saul's first offer to marry one of his daughters (1 Samuel 18:18).

⑬ אַחַר הַדְּבָרִים הָאֵלֶּה הָיָה דְּבַר יהוה אֶל אַבְרָם...

Abram _____ YHVH _____ _____ _____ after

Translation: "After these things, the word of the LORD came to Abram..."

Literal Translation: "After these things was the word of the LORD to Abram..."

Context: After Abram successfully rescued Lot from the four kings, and after Abram met with Melchizedek, the word of the LORD came to Abram in a vision (Genesis 15:1).

⑭ וַיִּקַּח עֵשָׂו אֶת נָשָׁיו וְאֶת בָּנָיו וְאֶת בְּנֹתָיו

his daughters _____ his sons _____ his wives _____ Esau and took

וְאֶת כָּל נַפְשׁוֹת בֵּיתוֹ...

_____ _____ _____ _____

Translation: "Esau took his wives, his sons, his daughters and all the persons of his household..."

Literal Translation: "Esau took his wives and his sons and his daughters and all the souls of his house..."

Context: Esau moved his entire household (with all his livestock and possessions) a distance away from his brother Jacob, because the land could not support both his and his brother's households (Genesis 36:6).

Exercise 3.4 - Let's Read Scripture! *continued...*

15) אֹהֲבֵי יהוה, שִׂנְאוּ רָע! שֹׁמֵר נַפְשׁוֹת

_____ _____ _____ hate YHVH _____

חֲסִידָיו מִיַּד רְשָׁעִים יַצִּילֵם.

he delivers _____ _____ his kind ones

Translation: "Those who love the LORD, hate evil! He guards the souls of His pious ones; from the hand of the wicked ones He delivers them."
Context: This psalm extols the reign of the Almighty and reminds the believer that God will judge the wicked and shine His light on the righteous (Psalm 97:10).

16) נַפְשִׁי יְשׁוֹבֵב יַנְחֵנִי בְמַעְגְּלֵי צֶדֶק לְמַעַן שְׁמוֹ.

_____ _____ righteousness in paths of he leads me he restores

Translation: "He restores my soul; He leads me in paths of righteousness for the sake of His name."
Context: These words are found in the famous Psalm which begins with "The LORD is my shepherd" (Psalm 23:3).

17) וַאֲנִי לֹא אָחוּס עַל נִינְוֵה, הָעִיר הַגְּדוֹלָה...

_____ _____ Nineveh _____ will pity _____ _____

Translation: "And shall I not show pity upon Nineveh, the great city..."
Context: The LORD replies to Jonah's anger in response to God's compassion for the city of Nineveh (Jonah 4:11).

18) וַיַּהֲפֹךְ אֵת הֶעָרִים הָאֵל וְאֵת כָּל הַכִּכָּר

the plain _____ _____ these _____ _____ he overthrew

וְאֵת כָּל יֹשְׁבֵי הֶעָרִים וְצֶמַח הָאֲדָמָה.

_____ and what grew _____ the dwellers of _____

Translation: "He overthrew these cities, and all the plain, and all those who dwelled in the cities, and what grew from the ground."
Context: The LORD's judgment against Sodom (Genesis 19:25).

Exercise 3.4 - Let's Read Scripture! *continued...*

⑲ ...לֹא הָיְתָה עִיר אֲשֶׁר הִשְׁלִימָה אֶל בְּנֵי יִשְׂרָאֵל

_____ ___ _____ made peace _____ _____ _____ _____

Translation: "There was not a city which made peace with the sons of Israel..."
Context: God hardened the hearts Israel's enemies so that none of them except the Hivites would make a peace treaty with Israel during Joshua's campaigns (Joshua 11:19).

⑳ ...בַּיָּמִים הָהֵם אֵין מֶלֶךְ בְּיִשְׂרָאֵל

_____ _____ _____ _____ _____ _____

Translation: "In those days [there was] no king in Israel..."
Context: During the time of the Judges, there were no kings in Israel (Judges 17:6).

㉑ ...וַיְהִי בַיָּמִים הָרַבִּים הָהֵם וַיָּמָת מֶלֶךְ מִצְרַיִם

_____ _____ died _____ _____ _____ and it was

Translation: "It was in [the course of] those many days [that] the king of Egypt died..."
Context: After Moses fled for his life from Pharaoh, many days passed, and during that time Pharaoh died (Exodus 2:23).

㉒ וּבְכָל אֶרֶץ מִצְרַיִם הָיָה לָחֶם.

bread* _____ _____ _____

Translation: "and in all the land of Egypt was bread..."
***Note:** This spelling uses an alternate vowel for the Hebrew word for *bread*.
Context: Because of Joseph's efforts to store food during the seven years of plenty, Egypt had food while the severe famine made all the surrounding lands destitute (Genesis 41:54).

㉓ מָה הַדָּבָר הַזֶּה אֲשֶׁר אַתָּה עֹשֶׂה לָעָם?

_____ _____ _____ _____ _____ _____ _____

Translation: "What [is] this thing which you are doing for the people?"
Context: Jethro asks Moses why he sits every day, morning until evening, to personally judge every dispute the people bring to him (Exodus 18:14).

Exercise 3.4 - Let's Read Scripture! *continued...*

(24) זֹאת   נַחֲלַת   מַטֵּה   בְּנֵי   יִשָּׂשכָר

_____   the inheritance of   of the tribe of   _____   Issachar

לְמִשְׁפְּחֹתָם,   הֶעָרִים   וְחַצְרֵיהֶן.

_____   _____   and their villages

Translation: "This [is] the inheritance of the tribe of the sons of Issachar according to their families; [these] cities and their villages."

Literal Translation: "This [is] the inheritance of the tribe of the sons of Issachar for/by their families; the cities and their villages."

Context: The description of the allotted portions of land given to each tribe (Joshua 19:23).

(25) תְּפִלָּה   לְמֹשֶׁה   אִישׁ   הָאֱלֹהִים.   אֲדֹנָי   מָעוֹן

_____   _____   _____   _____   a dwelling place

אַתָּה   הָיִיתָ   לָּנוּ   בְּדֹר   וָדֹר.

_____   _____   _____   _____

Translation: "A prayer of Moses, the man of God. Adonai, You have been a dwelling place for us throughout the generations."

Literal Translation: "A prayer [belonging] to Moses, the man of God. Adonai, a dwelling place You have been for us, in generation and generation."

Context: The psalmist reminds us that we rely day by day and moment by moment upon the mercies of God for our survival (Psalm 90:1).

(26) ...וְהֶעֱלָה   אֶתְכֶם   מִן   הָאָרֶץ   הַזֹּאת   אֶל   הָאָרֶץ   אֲשֶׁר

_____   _____   _____   _____   he will bring up

נִשְׁבַּע   לְאַבְרָהָם,   לְיִצְחָק,   וּלְיַעֲקֹב.

_____   _____   _____   he swore

Translation: "...he will bring you up from this land to the land which he swore (promised) to Abraham, to Isaac, and to Jacob."

Context: As Joseph was about to die, he told his brothers that God would surely bring the Israelites out of Egypt (Genesis 50:24).

Exercise 3.4 - Let's Read Scripture! *continued...*

㉗ ...כִּי בֵיתִי בֵּית תְּפִלָּה יִקָּרֵא לְכָל הָעַמִּים.

_____ _____ shall be called _____ _____ _____ _____

Translation: "...for My house will be called a house of prayer for all peoples."
Context: God promises that foreigners who love Him and keep his commandments will be accepted by Him. He describes "still others" who would be gathered, in addition to the exiles of Israel (Isaiah 56:7).

㉘ ...כֹּה אָמַר יהוה אֱלֹהֵי דָוִד אָבִיךָ

_____ _____ _____ YHVH _____ Thus

שָׁמַעְתִּי אֶת תְּפִלָּתֶךָ...

_____ _____ _____

Translation: "...thus said the LORD, the God of David your father: 'I have heard your prayer.'"
Context: After King Hezekiah prays that he might survive a fatal illness, God replies through the prophet Isaiah that He will heal him and will add fifteen years to his life (2 Kings 20:5).

㉙ וַיַּעֲזֹב אֶת יהוה אֱלֹהֵי אֲבֹתָיו וְלֹא הָלַךְ בְּדֶרֶךְ יהוה.

YHVH _____ _____ _____ his fathers _____ YHVH _____ he forsook

Translation: "He forsook the LORD, the God of his fathers, and did not walk in the way of the LORD."
Context: King Amon, son of Manasseh, did evil in the eyes of God, as his father had (2 Kings 21:22).

㉚ ...שְׁנֵי אֲנָשִׁים הָיוּ בְּעִיר אֶחָת...

one _____ _____ _____ two

Translation: "...two men were in one city..."
Context: These are the opening words of the parable about the rich man and the poor man which Nathan the prophet told David as he confronted David about his murder of Uriah the Hittite (2 Samuel 12:1).

Exercise 3.4 - Let's Read Scripture! *continued...*

(31) וְאָמַרְתָּ לְבִנְךָ, עֲבָדִים הָיִינוּ לְפַרְעֹה בְּמִצְרָיִם...

_____ to Pharaoh _____ _____ _____ and you will say

Translation: "Then you will say to your son, 'We were slaves to Pharaoh in Egypt...'"
Context: God tells his people that their sons will ask them the reason for the decrees and laws He gave them. These are the opening words of the response the fathers were to reply with (Deuteronomy 6:21).

(32) כֻּלָּנוּ כַּצֹּאן תָּעִינוּ; אִישׁ לְדַרְכּוֹ פָּנִינוּ...

we have turned _____ _____ have gone astray like sheep _____

Translation: "All of us, like sheep, have gone astray – each to his own way we have turned..."
Literal Translation: "All of us, like sheep, have gone astray – a man to his way we have turned..."
Context: The well-known Messianic passage regarding Yeshua, the Suffering Servant (Isaiah 53:6).

(33) בְּיוֹם הַשַּׁבָּת בְּיוֹם הַשַּׁבָּת יַעַרְכֶנּוּ לִפְנֵי יהוה

YHVH _____ he shall set _____ _____
it in order

תָּמִיד מֵאֵת בְּנֵי יִשְׂרָאֵל בְּרִית עוֹלָם.

_____ _____ _____ (from) _____

Translation: "Every sabbath day he shall set it in order before the LORD continually, an everlasting covenant from the children of Israel."
Literal Translation: "In the day of the sabbath, in the day of the sabbath, he shall set it in order before YHVH continually, from the sons of Israel a covenant everlasting."
Context: This passage refers to the "showbread" or "the bread of His presence" (Leviticus 24:8).

(34) וְהָיוּ עַל לֵב אַהֲרֹן בְּבֹאוּ לִפְנֵי יהוה וְנָשָׂא אַהֲרֹן

Aaron and shall bear YHVH _____ when Aaron _____ _____ they will be
he goes in

אֶת מִשְׁפַּט בְּנֵי יִשְׂרָאֵל עַל לִבּוֹ לִפְנֵי יהוה תָּמִיד.

_____ YHVH _____ _____ _____ judgment of _____

Translation: "And they shall be on the heart of Aaron when he goes in before the LORD, and Aaron shall carry the judgment of the sons of Israel on his heart before the LORD continually."
Context: The passage describes God's commandment for Aaron to keep the Urim and Thummim in the priestly breastpiece (Exodus 28:30).

מַעֲשֶׂה	זְמַן
אֲדָמָה	רָצוֹן
מִצְוָה	גְּאֻלָּה
נֶפֶשׁ	מִשְׁפָּחָה
תְּפִלָּה	עִיר

z'-MAHN time, season noun, masculine, singular (This word was introduced in Book 4, Lesson 3)	*mah-ah-SEH* deed, act noun, masculine, singular (This word was introduced in Book 4, Lesson 3)
rah-TSŌN will, favor noun, masculine, singular (This word was introduced in Book 4, Lesson 3)	*ah-dah-MAH* ground, land noun, feminine, singular (This word was introduced in Book 4, Lesson 3)
g'-oo-LAH redemption noun, feminine, singular (This word was introduced in Book 4, Lesson 3)	*mits-VAH* commandment noun, feminine, singular (This word was introduced in Book 4, Lesson 3)
mish-pah-CHAH family noun, feminine, singular (This word was introduced in Book 4, Lesson 3)	*NEH-fesh* soul noun, feminine, singular (This word was introduced in Book 4, Lesson 3)
eer city noun, feminine, singular (This word was introduced in Book 4, Lesson 3)	*t'-fih-LAH* prayer noun, feminine, singular (This word was introduced in Book 4, Lesson 3)

בְּרֵאשִׁית	דֶּרֶךְ
ג.א.ל	תָּמִיד
י.שׁ.ב	ה.י.ה
הָאֵלֶּה	הַזֶּה, הַזֹּאת
הָהֵם	הַהוּא, הַהִיא

DEH-rech
way, road

noun, common, singular

(This word was introduced in Book 4, Lesson 3)

b'-ray-SHEET
in the beginning

prepositional prefix + noun, feminine

(This word was introduced in Book 4, Lesson 3)

tah-MEED
always, continually

usually used as an adverb

(This word was introduced in Book 4, Lesson 3)

redeem

verb

(This word was introduced in Book 4, Lesson 3)

be

verb

(This word was introduced in Book 4, Lesson 3)

sit, dwell

verb

(This word was introduced in Book 4, Lesson 3)

hah-ZEH, ha-ZŌT
this

when used as an adjective modifying a singular definite noun; masculine and feminine forms

(This word was introduced in Book 4, Lesson 3)

ha-AY-leh
these

when used as an adjective modifying a plural definite noun; common form

(This word was introduced in Book 4, Lesson 3)

hah-HOO, ha-HEE
that

when used as an adjective modifying a singular definite noun; masculine and feminine forms

(This word was introduced in Book 4, Lesson 3)

ha-HAYM
those

when used as an adjective modifying a plural definite noun; masculine form

(This word was introduced in Book 4, Lesson 3)

Lesson 4: Adding Possessive Suffixes To Plural Nouns

That last lesson sure was a doozy. There were so many different concepts to cover, and that always means a lot more practice exercises are needed. To reward you for all that hard work and give you a break from the heavy stuff, we made this lesson very easy (and the end-of-lesson exercises will be *short*)!

In Book 2 of our series, we showed you how to add **possessive suffixes to *singular* nouns** (Lessons 6 and 7 of that book). For example, you learned how to take the Hebrew word for *house,* בַּיִת, change it to its "suffix-ready" form, -בֵּית, and then attach any one of ten possessive suffixes to show who *owns* the house. (Perhaps you'll recall the little "puzzle piece" graphics we employed to teach this concept.)   By the end of Lesson 7, you were able to create all ten possessive forms of this word in Hebrew; for example: *my house* בֵּיתִי, *his house* בֵּיתוֹ, *her house* בֵּיתָהּ, etc.

However, at that time we did <u>not</u> teach you how to add **possessive suffixes to *plural* nouns.** In other words, we never taught you how to say *my houses, his houses, her houses,* etc.   So, that's what this particular lesson will be about. You're ready for it now.

Before we start, though, we want to show you some wonderful new Biblical vocabulary.

			grace, favor*	*chayn*	ms	חֵן
places	*m'-ko-MŌT*	mp	מְקוֹמוֹת	place*	*mah-KŌM*	ms	מָקוֹם

*Important notes about the words above:

Biblical Hebrew has no plural form for the noun *grace/favor* חֵן.

The word *place* מָקוֹם is masculine but uses a feminine plural suffix. This word can have great spiritual importance, speaking on many occasions in scripture of a *place* which God has made holy, for example, or in which He has made a covenant with someone. It can carry the connotation of *a standing place* or *an established place,* coming as it does from the roots of the verb קוּם, *to arise, to stand up.*

Word List: Feminine Nouns

eyes	*ay-NAH-yim*	fp	עֵינַיִם	eye*	*AH-yin*	fs	עַיִן
				time*	*ayt*	fs	עֵת
				glory*	*tif-EH-ret*	fs	תִּפְאֶרֶת

*Important notes about the words above:

The singular word *eye* עַיִן is unusual in that it is stressed on the first syllable. Another way it is unusual is that, though it is feminine, the word receives a unique suffix that is not the ordinary feminine plural suffix.

The word *time* עֵת is found frequently in scripture (294 times) but only nine times in its plural form, so we're teaching only the singular form here. It means (usually) the time of a certain event or a particular time of day, but can also mean a "time period" or season.

The word *glory* תִּפְאֶרֶת occurs 51 times in scripture, in a variety of spellings. This word can appear with different vowels, so this particular spelling is just one of several. It does not have a plural form in Biblical Hebrew. Other possible translations include *beauty, splendor, honor, ornament, comeliness, majesty, boasting,* etc.

Word List: Verbs

know	י.ד.ע.
find	מ.צ.א.

Word List: Other Helpful Words

strong, mighty	*ghih-BOR*	גִּבּוֹר
as far as, until, up to	*ahd*	עַד

Adding Possessive Suffixes To Plural Nouns

You are ready to learn how to **add possessive suffixes to plural nouns.** As a review, let's look at some possessive suffixes on *singular* nouns first.

my son   בְּנִי

our father   אָבִינוּ

his glory   כְּבוֹדוֹ

If you want to add a possessive suffix to a *plural* noun, the first thing you need to do is take a look at that plural noun's suffix to see if it ends in *eem* (יִם) or *ōt* (וֹת).

If the noun ends in *eem* (יִם), then you need to **remove** that *eem* suffix entirely, and, in its place, attach the possessive suffix directly to the noun.

However, if the noun ends in *ōt* (וֹת), you will **keep** the *ōt* suffix and attach the possessive suffix right onto the existing *ōt* suffix.

One other important thing: **the possessive suffixes for plural nouns look *similar* to the ones for singular nouns, but they do have different vowels.** (On the next pages we will teach you all ten of these "possessive suffixes for plural nouns.")

Below are two examples of how to add possessive suffixes to plural nouns. The first example shows how to do this for a noun ending in *eem*. The second shows how to do it for a noun ending in *ōt*.

Adding A Possessive Suffix To A Noun Ending In *eem*

sons   בָּנִים

my sons   בָּנַי

Note that the *eem* ending has been **removed** and the possessive suffix for plural nouns which means "my" has been attached directly to the noun.

Adding A Possessive Suffix To A Noun Ending In *ōt*

commandments   מִצְוֺת

his commandments   מִצְוֺתָיו

Note that the *ōt* suffix has been **retained** and the possessive suffix for plural nouns which means "his" has been attached to the *ōt* suffix.

The Ten Possessive Suffixes For Nouns Ending In *eem*

בָּנִים

sons (plural noun, no possessive ending)

בָּנֵינוּ

our (c) sons*

בָּנַי

my (c) sons

בְּנֵיכֶם

your (mp) sons

בָּנֶיךָ

your (ms) sons*

בְּנֵיכֶן

your (fp) sons

בָּנַיִךְ

your (fs) sons*

בְּנֵיהֶם

their (m) sons

בָּנָיו

his sons

בְּנֵיהֶן

their (f) sons

בָּנֶיהָ

her sons*

You may notice a few minor vowel changes under the letters of the original noun as you study plural nouns with possessive suffixes. In this particular example, the *kah-matz* under the *bayt* changed to a *sh'vah* in the bottom left four forms.
*Please note that the forms with asterisks (*) are stressed on the second-to-the-last syllable rather than the final syllable.

The Ten Possessive Suffixes For Nouns Ending In *ōt*

daughters (plural noun, no possessive ending)

our (c) daughters*

my (c) daughters

your (mp) daughters

your (ms) daughters*

your (fp) daughters

your (fs) daughters*

their (m) daughters

his daughters

their (f) daughters

her daughters*

In this particular example, the *kah-matz* under the *bayt* changed to a *sh'vah* in all ten forms.
*Please note that the forms with asterisks * are emphasized on the second-to-the-last syllable rather than the final syllable.

A Comparison Of Possessive Suffixes For Singular Nouns And Plural Nouns Ending In *eem*

It is helpful to see the possessive endings for singular nouns side by side with those for plural nouns. Take a moment and visually compare the spelling differences between the two. Then, read them out loud and listen for differences, comparing one word from each column side by side.

words	דְּבָרִים	דָּבָר	word
my (c) words	דְּבָרַי	דְּבָרִי	my (c) word
your (ms) words	דְּבָרֶיךָ	דְּבָרְךָ	your (ms) word
your (fs) words	דְּבָרַיִךְ	דְּבָרֵךְ	your (fs) word
his words	דְּבָרָיו	דְּבָרוֹ	his word
her words	דְּבָרֶיהָ	דְּבָרָהּ	her word
our (c) words	דְּבָרֵינוּ	דְּבָרֵנוּ	our (c) word
your (mp) words	דִּבְרֵיכֶם	דְּבַרְכֶם	your (mp) word
your (fp) words	דִּבְרֵיכֶן	דְּבַרְכֶן	your (fp) word
their (m) words	דִּבְרֵיהֶם	דְּבָרָם	their (m) word
their (f) words	דִּבְרֵיהֶן	דְּבָרָן	their (f) word

A Comparison Of Possessive Suffixes For Singular Nouns And Plural Nouns Ending In *ōt*

Again, scan for spelling differences visually. Then read the columns aloud, listening for any differences in pronunciation.

commandments	מִצְוֹת	מִצְוָה	commandment
my (c) commandments	מִצְוֹתַי	מִצְוָתִי	my (c) commandment
your (ms) commandments	מִצְוֹתֶיךָ	מִצְוָתְךָ	your (ms) commandment
your (fs) commandments	מִצְוֹתַיִךְ	מִצְוָתֵךְ	your (fs) commandment
his commandments	מִצְוֹתָיו	מִצְוָתוֹ	his commandment
her commandments	מִצְוֹתֶיהָ	מִצְוָתָהּ	her commandment
our (c) commandments	מִצְוֹתֵינוּ	מִצְוָתֵנוּ	our (c) commandment
your (mp) commandments	מִצְוֹתֵיכֶם	מִצְוַתְכֶם	your (mp) commandment
your (fp) commandments	מִצְוֹתֵיכֶן	מִצְוַתְכֶן	your (fp) commandment
their (m) commandments	מִצְוֹתֵיהֶם	מִצְוָתָם	their (m) commandment
their (f) commandments	מִצְוֹתֵיהֶן	מִצְוָתָן	their (f) commandment

Exercise 4.1 - Riddle Review

Match each phrase or sentence to its translation, then write its circled "code letter" in the space provided. The circled letters will spell the answer to the riddle.

Who was the greatest stand-up comedian in the Bible?

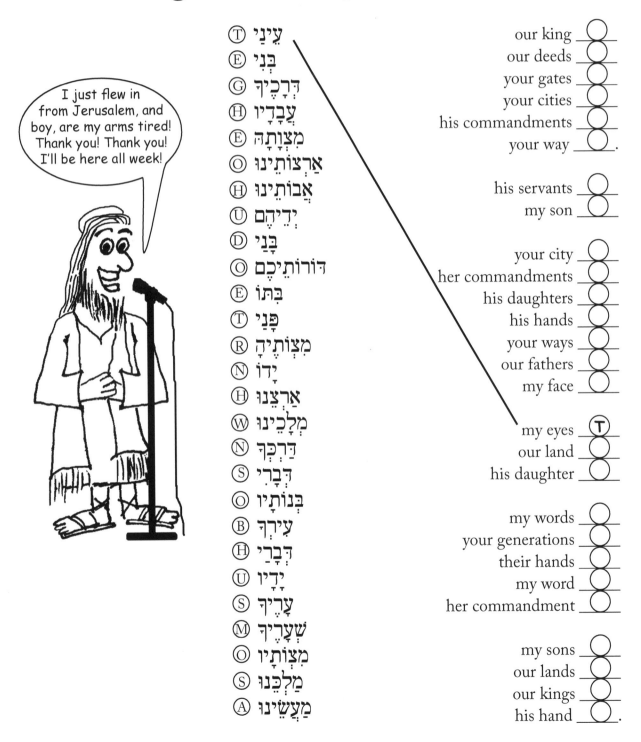

(T) עֵינִי

(E) בְּנִי

(G) דְּרָכֶיךָ

(H) עֲבָדָיו

(E) מִצְוֹתָהּ

(O) אַרְצוֹתֵינוּ

(H) אֲבוֹתֵינוּ

(U) יְדֵיהֶם

(D) בָּנַי

(O) דּוֹרוֹתֵיכֶם

(E) בִּתּוֹ

(T) פָּנַי

(R) מִצְוֹתֶיהָ

(N) יָדוֹ

(H) אַרְצֵנוּ

(W) מְלָכֵינוּ

(N) דַּרְכְּךָ

(S) דְּבָרַי

(O) בְּנוֹתָיו

(B) עִירְךָ

(H) דְּבָרֶיךָ

(U) יָדָיו

(S) עָרֶיךָ

(M) שְׁעָרֶיךָ

(O) מִצְוֹתָיו

(S) מַלְכֵּנוּ

(A) מַעֲשֵׂינוּ

our king ◯◯

our deeds ◯◯

your gates ◯◯

your cities ◯◯

his commandments ◯◯

your way ◯ .

his servants ◯◯

my son ◯(T)

your city ◯◯

her commandments ◯◯◯

his daughters ◯◯◯

his hands ◯◯◯

your ways ◯◯◯

our fathers ◯◯◯

my face ◯◯◯

my eyes (T)◯

our land ◯◯

his daughter ◯◯

my words ◯◯

your generations ◯◯

their hands ◯◯

my word ◯◯

her commandment ◯◯

my sons ◯◯

our lands ◯◯

our kings ◯◯

his hand ◯ .

Answer: Samson. He brought the house down.

Lesson 4 Flashcards

	חֵן
מָקוֹם	עַיִן
עֵת	תִּפְאֶרֶת
י.ד.ע	מ.צ.א
גִּבּוֹר	עַד

chayn
grace, favor
noun, masculine, singular

(This word was introduced in Book 4, Lesson 4)

mah-KŌM
place
noun, masculine, singular

(This word was introduced in Book 4, Lesson 4)

AH-yin
eye
noun, feminine, singular

(This word was introduced in Book 4, Lesson 4)

ayt
time
noun, feminine, singular

(This word was introduced in Book 4, Lesson 4)

tif-EH-ret
glory
noun, feminine, singular

(This word was introduced in Book 4, Lesson 4)

know
verb

(This word was introduced in Book 4, Lesson 4)

find
verb

(This word was introduced in Book 4, Lesson 4)

ghih-BOR
strong, mighty
adjective

(This word was introduced in Book 4, Lesson 4)

ahd
as far as, until, up to

(This word was introduced in Book 4, Lesson 4)

Lesson 5:
The Future Tense

Let's begin this lesson by reviewing all the things you already know about verbs. Here are three facts regarding Hebrew verbs:

1. Verbs are formed by adding patterns of vowels or other letters to **root letters,** which look like:

say א.מ.ר

2. The **participle** of a verb is formed by adding the **participle pattern** to the root letters. Example:

saying (ms) אוֹמֵר

3. The **past tense** of a verb is formed by adding the **past tense pattern** to the root letters. Example:

I said אָמַרְתִּי

It's as simple as that. The good news is that the future tense is just as simple. It's only a matter of adding the future tense pattern to the root letters. We will teach you this pattern in this lesson, and it will be a brief lesson. But first, here's more Biblical vocabulary.

Word List: Masculine Nouns

			seed, offspring*	*zeh-RAH*	ms		זֶרַע
			strength*	*ōz*	ms		עֹז
multitudes	*ts'-vah-ŌT*	mp	צְבָאוֹת	multitude*	*tsah-VAH*	ms	צָבָא
rocks	*tsoo-REEM*	mp	צוּרִים	rock	*tsoor*	ms	צוּר

*The words *seed* זֶרַע and *strength* עֹז don't have plural forms in Biblical Hebrew, although *seed* זֶרַע may be understood as either singular or plural, depending on context. *Multitude,* צָבָא, may also be translated "host." Its plural form takes an unusual feminine suffix. This word is famously used in scripture in the phrase "LORD of hosts."

Word List: Feminine Nouns

tasks	m'-lah-CHŌT fp	מְלָאכוֹת	work, task*	m'-lah-CHAH fs	מְלָאכָה
souls, spirits	n'-shah-MŌT fp	נְשָׁמוֹת	soul, breath, spirit*	n'shah-MAH fs	נְשָׁמָה

*Important notes about the words above:

The word *task, work* מְלָאכָה is also translated *occupation, duty* or *craftsmanship*. The word is also used in the scripture to refer to God's *work:* "He rested from His *work* of creation" (Gen. 2:3). This word looks and sounds a lot like words relating to *king* and *kingdom*, but don't be fooled by this. There is an additional root letter *aleph* א which differentiates this word from any of those related to royalty. Do you remember your vocabulary for *angels/messengers*, מַלְאָכִים ? The word *task, work* מְלָאכָה originates from the exact same root, as the angels carry out all the *work* or *tasks* that the LORD assigns.

You may be wondering how the word *soul, breath, spirit* נְשָׁמָה differs from the word *soul* נֶפֶשׁ which you learned in prior lessons. They are usually translated similarly when used in similar contexts, but נְשָׁמָה has its roots in the verb נ.שׁ.מ which means to *gasp* or to *pant*, and expresses itself in the noun form as the *breath of life, the breath of God, the breath of man,* or *every breathing thing.* By extension, it is used to convey the concept of the *soul* or *spirit.* The Hebrew word נֶפֶשׁ, on the other hand, is from a different root, and it carries the meaning of *the innermost living part* of an individual, and can express things such as *the seat of the emotions/passions/desires, one's spiritual appetite (hunger/thirst), the life of a living being which resides in the blood,* or *that innermost part which makes an individual an individual.*

Another Useful Word

after, behind	ah-CHAR, ah-chah-RAY	אַחַר , אַחֲרֵי

This word appears 715 times in scripture, so it is a useful word to know! It literally means *the hindmost portion* or *the following part.* This can apply to positions in place or in time, for example, "I establish My covenant with you, and with your descendants *after* you" (Genesis 9:9); "*After* the flood, Noah lived 350 years" (Genesis 9:28); "The pillar of cloud also moved from in front and stood *behind* them (Exodus 14:19). Spiritually, this word also can imply *pursuit* of either wickedness or holiness, as in *chasing after* or *following after* these things. **One of the most useful things about this word is that it can either "stand alone"** (in either of the two spellings above), **or it can have pronominal suffixes attached,** just like many of the prepositions you learned earlier. Here are a few examples of this word with pronominal suffixes attached:

after us אַחֲרֵינוּ	after her אַחֲרֶיהָ	after you אַחֲרֶיךָ

after me אַחֲרַי	after them אַחֲרֵיהֶם

The Flexible Meaning Of The Future Tense

Before we learn the pattern for the future tense, there is one very important thing you need to know. The future tense of a Hebrew verb can carry the meaning of **an action that takes place in the future**, *or* **an action that one *desires* to take place in the future.** The same exact Hebrew verb form can express either idea, or both ideas!

English verbs do not have this flexibility within the verb itself. Instead, English verbs use different helping verbs to augment the main verb in order to get across different meanings. Let's use the verb "reign" as an example. Notice the use of the helper verbs *will, shall,* and *may.*

He **will reign** forever.	indicates a future action.
He **shall reign** forever.	indicates a future action.
May he **reign** forever.	indicates a *desire* for the future action to occur.

Compare this, now, to the Hebrew verb *reign* in the future tense:

he will reign *or*	
he shall reign *or*	יִמְלֹךְ
may he reign	

The Hebrew future tense verb in the example above can mean *all three* of those things. The translator must study the context carefully to choose the correct translation.

In certain cases, **the context makes both meanings true simultaneously.**   For example, a prophet may speak to the sons of Israel using the future tense *you will sanctify.* This may be interpreted, "You will sanctify His name" as a word of prophecy about a future event which is certain to occur. It also may be interpreted, "May you sanctify His name" as a desire for that future action to occur. In a case like this, both may be true simultaneously. The prophet may *pray aloud* in faith for this action to occur one day, while also *prophesying* in faith, knowing this future action to be a certainty. Those of you who have received a word of promise from the Holy Spirit – and then prayed fervently in agreement with that word – will have experienced this dual phenomenon first hand.

For the sake of brevity, our answer keys throughout this book will translate the majority of the answers with the simple future tense: **an action that takes place in the future.** However, in your own translation work, you should **always keep in mind the flexible meaning of the future tense.**

The next page shows the pattern for the future tense.

The Pattern For The Future Tense

rule, reign

I will rule, 1cs

we will rule, 1cp

you will rule, 2ms

you will rule, 2mp

you will rule, 2fs

you will rule, 2fp

he will rule, 3ms

they will rule, 3mp

she will rule, 3fs

they will rule, 3fp

Notice the unusual phenomenon that the 2ms and 3fs forms are spelled identically. So are the 2fp and 3fp forms. All forms are stressed on the final syllable, except for the 2fp and 3fp forms, which are stressed on the second syllable.

An Example Of The Pattern Applied To Another Verb

Here's how the pattern is applied to the verb שׁ.מ.ר *guard*.

we (c) will guard	נִשְׁמֹר	I (c) will guard	אֶשְׁמֹר
you (mp) will guard	תִּשְׁמְרוּ	you (ms) will guard	תִּשְׁמֹר
you (fp) will guard	תִּשְׁמֹרְנָה	you (fs) will guard	תִּשְׁמְרִי
they (m) will guard	יִשְׁמְרוּ	he will guard	יִשְׁמֹר
they (f) will guard	תִּשְׁמֹרְנָה	she will guard	תִּשְׁמֹר

Certain Verbs Vary *Slightly* From The Pattern

As you might expect, there are slight deviations from the pattern when it comes to certain verbs. In the case of the verb שׁ.מ.ע *hear*, for example, the vowel under the second root letter changes from a *chō-lam* (ֹ) to a *pah-tach* (ַ). This is a very tiny change, but one you need to be aware of.

we (c) will hear	נִשְׁמַע	I (c) will hear	אֶשְׁמַע
you (mp) will hear	תִּשְׁמְעוּ	you (ms) will hear	תִּשְׁמַע
you (fp) will hear	תִּשְׁמַעְנָה	you (fs) will hear	תִּשְׁמְעִי
they (m) will hear	יִשְׁמְעוּ	he will hear	יִשְׁמַע
they (f) will hear	תִּשְׁמַעְנָה	she will hear	תִּשְׁמַע

Lots of other verbs will have this particular slight deviation. Here's a list of the verbs you know so far which fall into this category:

choose	ב.ח.ר
trust	ב.ט.ח
redeem	ג.א.ל
hear	שׁ.מ.ע
find	מ.צ.א

Irregular Future Tense Forms You Should Know

Finally, there are certain verbs which vary *greatly* from the usual pattern – so much so that they fall into the category of "irregular." Two of these verbs are used quite a bit in scripture; we gave you *all* their forms below. However, we advise that you not try to memorize *all* ten forms for these verbs right now, because eight of their forms appear relatively few times in the Bible, whereas two of their forms appear a *lot*. **We have highlighted the forms that appear most frequently in scripture. Focus on memorizing just the highlighted forms below,** and your ability to read much of scripture will increase immediately by leaps and bounds. Later on down the road, you can always come back to this list and memorize *all* the forms, if you so desire.

א.מ.ר *say*

we (c) will say	נֹאמַר	*I (c) will say*	אֹמַר
you (mp) will say	תֹּאמְרוּ	*you (ms) will say*	תֹּאמַר
you (fp) will say	תֹּאמַרְנָה	*you (fs) will say*	תֹּאמְרִי
they (m) will say	יֹאמְרוּ	*he will say*	יֹאמַר
they (f) will say	תֹּאמַרְנָה	*she will say*	תֹּאמַר

ע.שׂ.ה *make/do*

we (c) will make/do	נַעֲשֶׂה	*I (c) will make/do*	אֶעֱשֶׂה
you (mp) will make/do	תַּעֲשׂוּ	*you (ms) will make/do*	תַּעֲשֶׂה
you (fp) will make/do	תַּעֲשֶׂינָה	*you (fs) will make/do*	תַּעֲשִׂי
they (m) will make/do	יַעֲשׂוּ	*he will make/do*	יַעֲשֶׂה
they (f) will make/do	תַּעֲשֶׂינָה	*she will make/do*	תַּעֲשֶׂה

Exercise 5.1 - Crossword Review

Write the English translation for each Hebrew word below.

Across

2. מְלָאכָה

3. זֶרַע

5. צוּר

6. צָבָא

Down

1. נְשָׁמָה

3. עֹז

4. אַחֲרֵי

Answers 5.1 - Crossword Review

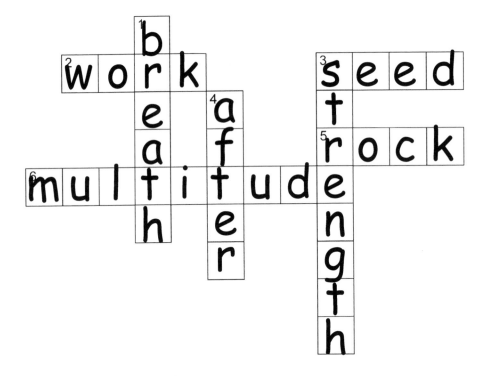

Across

2. מְלָאכָה

3. זֶרַע

5. צוּר

6. צָבָא

Down

1. נְשָׁמָה

3. עֹז

4. אַחֲרֵי

Exercise 5.2 - Translation Practice

Translate each phrase into English. *Hint: Each line will have a verb in participle (present) form, in past tense form, and in future tense form, though not necessarily in that order.* **Specify the gender and/or number** for any forms that turn out to be ambiguous in English translation; for example, "you (mp) walked."

① אַתָּה מֶלֶךְ _____ מָלַכְתָּ _____ תִּמְלֹךְ _____

② יֵשׁוּעַ יִמְלֹךְ _____ מָלַךְ _____ הוּא מוֹלֵךְ _____

③ שָׂרָה שָׁמְרָה _____ הִיא שֹׁמֶרֶת _____ תִּשְׁמֹר _____

④ אָנוּ גּוֹאֲלִים _____ גָּאַלְנוּ _____ נִגְאַל _____

⑤ אֶכְתֹּב _____ אֲנִי כּוֹתֵב _____ כָּתַבְתִּי _____

⑥ שָׁמְעוּ _____ יִשְׁמְעוּ _____ הֵם שׁוֹמְעִים _____

⑦ הֵם מֹצְאִים _____ מָצְאוּ _____ יִמְצְאוּ _____

Answers 5.2 - Translation Practice

It's perfectly fine if any of your future tense answers used translations of *desired* action; i.e., "may they hear" rather than the simple future certainty of "they shall hear." Both are valid. Also, you may have chosen the word "listen," rather than "hear." Your participle translations may have been simple present tense form ("he hears"), or the *-ing* form ("he is hearing"). Each translation in our answer key represents merely one of several correct answers; we just went with whatever random choice came to mind.

① אַתָּה מֶלֶךְ __you (ms) rule__ מָלַכְתָּ __you (ms) ruled__ תִּמְלֹךְ __you (ms) will rule__

② יֵשׁוּעַ יִמְלֹךְ __Yeshua will rule__ מָלַךְ __he ruled__ הוּא מוֹלֵךְ __he rules/is ruling__

③ שָׂרָה שָׁמְרָה __Sarah guarded__ הִיא שֹׁמֶרֶת __she guards__ תִּשְׁמֹר __she will guard__

④ אָנוּ גּוֹאֲלִים __we are redeeming__ גָּאַלְנוּ __we redeemed__ נִגְאַל __we shall redeem__

⑤ אֶכְתֹּב __I will write__ אֲנִי כּוֹתֵב __I (m) am writing__ כָּתַבְתִּי __I wrote__

⑥ שָׁמְעוּ __they (m) heard__ יִשְׁמְעוּ __they (m) will hear__ הֵם שׁוֹמְעִים __they (m) hear__

⑦ הֵם מֹצְאִים __they (m) find__ מָצְאוּ __they (m) found__ יִמְצְאוּ __may they (m) find__

Exercise 5.3 - Scripture Phrases

Each phrase contains a verb in the future tense. **Translate each phrase into English. Specify the gender and/or number** for forms that turn out to be ambiguous in English translation; i.e., "you (mp) walked." We have provided translations for any words you have not been taught yet.

Regarding a false prophet (Deut. 13:3)

① ...לֹא תִשְׁמַע אֶל דִּבְרֵי הַנָּבִיא הַהוּא

From the song of Moses and Miriam (Ex. 15:18)

② יְהוָה יִמְלֹךְ לְעֹלָם וָעֶד.
   YHVH

God's words to Abraham (Gen. 17:9)

③ ...וְאַתָּה אֶת בְּרִיתִי תִשְׁמֹר, אַתָּה וְזַרְעֲךָ אַחֲרֶיךָ לְדֹרֹתָם.

Hosea prophesies Israel's coming chastisement (Hos. 10:3)

④ ...יֹאמְרוּ אֵין מֶלֶךְ לָנוּ...

God tells Moses He will replace the broken stone tablets (Deut. 10:2)

⑤ וְאֶכְתֹּב עַל הַלֻּחֹת אֶת הַדְּבָרִים אֲשֶׁר הָיוּ עַל הַלֻּחֹת הָרִאשֹׁנִים.
       first   *the tablets*   *the tablets*

Answers 5.3 - Scripture Phrases

Some of the answers below are followed by a more literal translation (in italics), to help you check your work.

1. You (ms) will not listen to the words of that prophet...

2. The LORD shall reign forever and ever.

3. ...and you (ms) will keep My covenant, you and your offspring after you throughout their generations.
   ...and you, My covenant you shall keep, you and your seed after you for their generations.

4. ...they (m) will say, we have no king...
   ...they will say, there is no king for us...

5. And I will write on the tablets the words which were on the first tablets.

Lesson 5 Flashcards

By now, you will have noticed that we are no longer providing flashcards for all forms of the verbs which we introduce, mainly because there would end up being so many cards... but also because flashcards won't serve you as well as just being able to recognize the patterns themselves.   So, we will only give you the root letters of each verb to memorize on your flashcards. If you can recognize the root letters of a given verb, and if you can recognize the pattern the verb is using, you will always be able to translate it.

	זָרַע
צָבָא	עֹז
מְלָאכָה	צוּר
אַחַר, אַחֲרֵי	נְשָׁמָה

zeh-RAH

seed, offspring

noun, masculine, singular

(This word was introduced in Book 4, Lesson 5)

ōz

strength

noun, masculine, singular

(This word was introduced in Book 4, Lesson 5)

---

tsah-VAH

multitude, host

noun, masculine, singular

(This word was introduced in Book 4, Lesson 5)

---

tsoor

rock

noun, masculine, singular

(This word was introduced in Book 4, Lesson 5)

---

m'-lah-CHAH

work, task

noun, feminine, singular

(This word was introduced in Book 4, Lesson 5)

---

n'shah-MAH

soul, breath, spirit

noun, feminine, singular

(This word was introduced in Book 4, Lesson 5)

---

ah-CHAR,
ah-chah-RAY

after, behind

(This word was introduced in Book 4, Lesson 5)

Lesson 6:
The Reversing Vav (וֹ)

Earlier in this book, we mentioned that we would eventually teach you an alternative way to represent the past tense. The time has come. This lesson will show you a fascinating way that **the letter *vav* can be used to "reverse" the tense of a verb**... from past to future, and from future to past! This phenomenon is really interesting and will make your translation work much more fun because of the flexibility in meaning that it introduces.

Before we begin, let's get to know some more Hebrew words from the Bible!

Word List: Masculine Nouns

mornings	*b'kah-REEM*	mp	בְּקָרִים		morning*	*BŌ-ker*	ms	בֹּקֶר
sins	*chah-tah-EEM*	mp	חֲטָאִים		sin*	*chayt*	ms	חֵטְא
evenings	*ah-rah-VEEM*	mp	עֲרָבִים		evening	*EH-rev*	ms	עֶרֶב

*Important notes about the words above:

The word *morning* בֹּקֶר is emphasized on the first syllable.

The noun *sin* חֵטְא has its roots in a verb ח.ט.א which means *miss the mark, miss the way, miss the goal, commit an error, make a mistake, sin.*

fear, awe*	*yir-AH*	fs	יִרְאָה
help*	*ez-RAH*	fs	עֶזְרָה

*Important notes about the words above:

The word *fear, awe* יִרְאָה does not have a plural form. It is also translated *dread* or *reverence,* and is often applied in the sense of "fear of God."

The noun *help* עֶזְרָה does not have a plural form. It has its roots in a verb עֶ.ז.ר which means *help, aid.* These same root letters are found in the Hebrew name "Ezra."

A Common Gender Noun

signs	*ō-TŌT*	cp	אוֹתוֹת	sign	*ōt*	cs	אוֹת

In scripture, this word appears in either masculine or feminine gender. The genders of the surrounding words usually make it possible to determine which gender is in use. The plural form takes the *ōt* ending. This versatile word can denote *a sign in the heavens* (moon, stars, etc.), *a mark on a man* (such as Cain's mark, or the "mark" of circumcision), *a sign of things to come* (proof of the truth of a prophecy), *an outward token of a covenant* (rainbow, circumcision, etc), or *a miraculous sign* displaying God's power (plagues in Egypt, etc.).

Word List: Verbs

sin	ח.ט.א
forgive*	ס.ל.ח
help*	עֶ.ז.ר
rest, cease (i.e., from working)	שׁ.ב.ת

*The verbs *forgive* ס.ל.ח and *help* עֶ.ז.ר are usually followed by the preposition *to/for* (לְ).

Yeshua forgave us and helped us. יֵשׁוּעַ סָלַח לָנוּ וְעָזַר לָנוּ.

Ladies And Gentlemen:
The Great, The Wonderful, The Mysterious...
Reversing *Vav!*

By now, you're familiar with the letter *vav* ו used as a prefix. When it is placed at the beginning of a word, it is translated *"and."* Since *"and"* is a *conjunction*, and the *vav* ו is attached as a *prefix*, we would say that the letter *vav* ו is acting here as a **conjunctive prefix.**

Abraham **and** Isaac   אַבְרָהָם וְיִצְחָק

If the letter *vav* had hands, then any time he was doing his job as a conjunctive prefix, he might be holding up a sign that said *"and."*

However, this is only a part-time job for the *vav*. He also has another part-time job.

The *vav* has a secret hidden talent, which he uses on his other job. He works as a part-time magician, performing tricks at parties with his Magical Wand of Time Travel. For his magic gigs, he calls himself "The Great, Wonderful And Mysterious Reversing Vav." (We think this is a bit much, so we just refer to him as the *reversing vav.)*

When the *vav* is attached to a verb as a *reversing vav*, he changes the tense of the verb. **If a verb is written in the <u>past tense</u> form and has a reversing *vav* attached, it is translated as a <u>future tense</u> verb.**

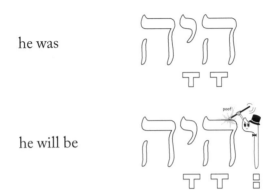

Likewise, **if a verb is written in the <u>future tense</u> form and has a reversing *vav* attached, it is translated as a <u>past tense</u> verb.**

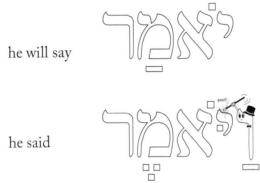

You may have noticed in this particular example that the *vav's* powerful Wand of Time Travel also changed a vowel and added a dot. Such slight changes may occur during these tense reversals. Nothing to be alarmed about.

A Vav Prefix On A Verb Isn't ALWAYS A Reversing Vav

Just because a *vav* is attached to the beginning of a verb doesn't mean it is acting in a *reversing vav* role. Sometimes, the *vav* is just doing its other job as a *conjunctive prefix*. For example, if you wanted to say the phrase "he walked and he guarded," you would need to be able to use the *vav* as a conjunctive prefix, but *without* reversing the tense. In this situation, our *vav* needs to do his other part-time job, holding up his *"and"* sign.

he walked and he guarded

"Now, just you wait a darn tootin' minute!" you say. "How in the world are we supposed to know which job the *vav* is doing in the Hebrew scriptures? That letter is not going to be holding any signs or wearing any top hats in the Bible!" The answer to your very astute observation is, "You'll need to use the context." Most of the time, it's clear from the situation whether the *vav* is intended to reverse the tense or to act as a conjunction.

The Multitasking Vav

If you're feeling a bit miffed over the fact that the *vav* can change jobs without warning, get ready for this one. The *vav* can actually <u>multitask</u>. That's right. **The *vav* can do *both* functions at once: it can act as a conjunctive prefix while simultaneously reversing the tense of the verb that follows it.** Here's a picture of our little friend doing *both* jobs at once. Just look at him go!

What would this look like in scripture? The *vav* highlighted below is doing both jobs at once.

| it | and you shall keep *reversing vav changes past tense to future tense, but also acts as a conjunction "and"* | the Sabbath | d.o.m. | you shall remember *reversing vav changes past tense to future tense* |

The Future Tense Of The Verb "Be" ה.י.ה

One last thing we need to go over with you before we let you get to the exercises. The verb *be* ה.י.ה has unusal forms in the future tense (as you probably guessed). We're going to give you a list of all ten forms, but **please just memorize the two forms we highlighted rather than the whole list,** because those two forms are the ones you will see most often in scripture.

be ה.י.ה

we (c) will be	נִהְיֶה	*I (c) will be*	אֶהְיֶה
you (mp) will be	תִּהְיוּ	*you (ms) will be*	תִּהְיֶה
you (fp) will be	תִּהְיֶינָה	*you (fs) will be*	תִּהְיִי
they (m) will be	יִהְיוּ	*he/it will be*	יִהְיֶה
they (f) will be	תִּהְיֶינָה	*she/it will be*	תִּהְיֶה

A Special Form To Memorize: וַיְהִי

If you take the form יִהְיֶה from the list above (which means *he/it will be*) and put a reversing *vav* in front of it, it reverses tense and changes to an unusual shortened spelling, וַיְהִי which means *he/it was*. It often gets used in scripture like this: "**And it was** that God spoke to Moses." Since this sounds a bit unnatural in English, translators often take the liberty of translating this form *"and it came to pass,"* as in, "**And it came to pass** that God spoke to Moses."

Exercise 6.1 - Crossword Review

Write the English translation for each Hebrew word below.

Across

1. עֶזְרָה
6. ס.ל.ח
7. יִרְאָה
8. אוֹת

Down

2. עֶרֶב
3. בֹּקֶר
4. ח.ט.א
5. שׁ.ב.ת

Answers 6.1 - Crossword Review

Across

1. עֶזְרָה
6. ס.ל.ח
7. יִרְאָה
8. אוֹת

Down

2. עֶרֶב
3. בֹּקֶר
4. ח.ט.א
5. שׁ.ב.ת

Exercise 6.2 - Translation Practice

Translate each verb into each of its possible three translations, writing them under the appropriate column heading. The first line is done for you as an example.

vav as a conjunctive prefix + reversing *vav*	reversing *vav*	*vav* as a conjunctive prefix (not reversing)	
and he will do	he will do	and he did	וְעָשָׂה
			וַיִּמְלֹךְ ①
			וְסָלַחְנוּ ②
			וְשָׁבַתְנוּ ③
			וְהָיוּ ④
			וַיִּהְיוּ ⑤
			וְחָטְאוּ ⑥
			וְשָׁמַעְתִּי ⑦
			וַיִּבְחֲרוּ ⑧
			וְשָׁמְרוּ ⑨

Answers 6.2 - Translation Practice

vav as a conjunctive prefix + reversing vav	reversing vav	vav as a conjunctive prefix (not reversing)		
and he will do	he will do	and he did	וְעָשָׂה	
and he ruled	he ruled	and he will rule	וַיִּמְלֹךְ	①
and we will forgive	we will forgive	and we forgave	וְסָלַחְנוּ	②
and we will rest	we will rest	and we rested	וְשָׁבַתְנוּ	③
and they will be	they will be	and they were	וְהָיוּ	④
and they were	they were	and they will be	וַיִּהְיוּ	⑤
and they will sin	they will sin	and they sinned	וְחָטְאוּ	⑥
and I will hear	I will hear	and I heard	וְשָׁמַעְתִּי	⑦
and they chose	they chose	and they will choose	וַיִּבְחֲרוּ	⑧
and they will guard	they will guard	and they guarded	וְשָׁמְרוּ	⑨

Exercise 6.3 - Scripture Phrases

Translate each phrase into English. You'll need to use the context to determine whether any of the *vavs* are reversing *vavs*. Also, we have provided translations below words you haven't been taught yet.

From the account of Creation (Genesis 1:3)

① וַיֹּאמֶר אֱלֹהִים יְהִי אוֹר, וַיְהִי אוֹר.

let be

Noah's prophecy over Canaan, the son of Ham (Genesis 9:25)

② וַיֹּאמֶר, אָרוּר כְּנָעַן - עֶבֶד עֲבָדִים יִהְיֶה לְאֶחָיו.

to his brothers   *Canaan*   *cursed*

God's words to the Israelites (Exodus 31:14)

③ וּשְׁמַרְתֶּם אֶת הַשַּׁבָּת כִּי קֹדֶשׁ הוּא לָכֶם...

it

Moses restates God's commandments as Israel prepares to enter the promised land (Deuteronomy 16:12)

④ וְזָכַרְתָּ כִּי עֶבֶד הָיִיתָ בְּמִצְרָיִם, וְשָׁמַרְתָּ וְעָשִׂיתָ אֶת הַחֻקִּים הָאֵלֶּה.

statutes

Leah conceives and gives birth to a son (Genesis 30:17)

⑤ וַיִּשְׁמַע אֱלֹהִים אֶל לֵאָה, וַתַּהַר וַתֵּלֶד לְיַעֲקֹב בֵּן, חֲמִישִׁי.

the fifth   *and bore*   *and she conceived*

Answers To Exercises On This Page

1. And God said, "Let [there] be light." And [there] was light.
2. He said, "Cursed is Canaan – a servant of servants he shall be to his brothers."
3. You shall keep the Sabbath, for it is holy to you...
4. You shall remember that you were a slave in Egypt, and you shall keep and do these statutes.
5. God listened to Leah and she conceived and bore to Jacob a son, the fifth.

Exercise 6.3 - Scripture Phrases, *continued*

The Israelites ask Moses to pray that God remove the venomous snakes (Numbers 21:7)

⑥ וַיָּבֹא הָעָם אֶל מֹשֶׁה, וַיֹּאמְרוּ, חָטָאנוּ, כִּי דִבַּרְנוּ בַיהוה...
came   *against YHVH*

God rests on the seventh day (Genesis 2:2)

⑦ וַיְכַל אֱלֹהִים בַּיּוֹם הַשְּׁבִיעִי מְלַאכְתּוֹ אֲשֶׁר עָשָׂה – וַיִּשְׁבֹּת בַּיּוֹם
the seventh   *finished*

הַשְּׁבִיעִי מִכָּל מְלַאכְתּוֹ אֲשֶׁר עָשָׂה.
the seventh

Moses relates God's commandment to love the Lord (Deuteronomy 6:5)

⑧ וְאָהַבְתָּ אֵת יהוה אֱלֹהֶיךָ בְּכָל לְבָבְךָ, וּבְכָל נַפְשְׁךָ, וּבְכָל מְאֹדֶךָ.
your might   *YHVH*

God's words to the Israelites through Moses (Leviticus 20:26)

⑨ וִהְיִיתֶם לִי קְדֹשִׁים, כִּי קָדוֹשׁ אֲנִי יהוה...
YHVH

Answers To Exercises On This Page

6. The people came to Moses and said, "We have sinned, for we have spoken against the Lord."

7. God finished on the seventh day His work which He had made – and He rested on the seventh day from all His work which He had made.

8. And you shall love the Lord your God with all your heart, and with all your soul, and with all your might.

9. You shall be holy to me, for I, the Lord, [am] holy.

Exercise 6.3 - Scripture Phrases, *continued*

Moses prays for God to forgive the people's sin (Exodus 32:32)

⑩ וְעַתָּה, אִם תִּשָּׂא חַטָּאתָם – וְאִם אַיִן מְחֵנִי נָא, מִסִּפְרְךָ אֲשֶׁר כָּתַבְתָּ.

and now   if   you will forgive   but if   not   blot me   please

---

Moses instructs the elders to write the Torah on large stones after they cross the Jordan (Deut. 27:3)

⑪ וְכָתַבְתָּ עֲלֵיהֶן אֶת כָּל דִּבְרֵי הַתּוֹרָה הַזֹּאת...

Moses appoints judges over the people (Exodus 18:25)

⑫ וַיִּבְחַר מֹשֶׁה אַנְשֵׁי חַיִל מִכָּל יִשְׂרָאֵל וַיִּתֵּן אֹתָם רָאשִׁים עַל הָעָם...

heads   ability   men of

God gives the rainbow as the sign of His covenant with the earth (Genesis 9:13)

⑬ אֶת קַשְׁתִּי נָתַתִּי בֶּעָנָן, וְהָיְתָה לְאוֹת בְּרִית בֵּינִי וּבֵין הָאָרֶץ.

in the cloud   my rainbow

God commands Israel to keep His words on their heart (Deuteronomy 6:6)

⑭ וְהָיוּ הַדְּבָרִים הָאֵלֶּה, אֲשֶׁר אָנֹכִי מְצַוְּךָ הַיּוֹם, עַל לְבָבֶךָ.

I command you

Answers To Exercises On This Page

10. And now, if You will forgive their sin – but if not, please blot me from Your book which You have written.

11. And you shall write on them all the words of this Torah...

12. Moses chose men of ability from all Israel and gave them (i.e., *made them*) heads over the people.

13. My rainbow I have given in the cloud, and it shall be for a token of the covenant between Me and the earth.

14. And these words which I am commanding you today shall be upon your heart.

    Literal translation: *And shall be these words, which I command you today, upon your heart.*

A Word Of Encouragement

We want to stop right here and tell you how proud of you we are – proud that you have completed this series to this point! Take a moment and think. Do you remember those days, back in Book 1, when you couldn't even tell an *alef* from a *tav*? Those days weren't so very long ago! Now, glance back at the last three pages you have just completed. Can you believe that you are reading entire phrases of scripture with very little assistance? And those exercises were *not* easy. In fact, they were extremely challenging, weren't they?

Let's review all the things you have learned about Biblical Hebrew so far:

- Nouns (masculine, feminine, common, singular, plural, absolute and construct form)

- The Definite Article "The"; This, These, That, and Those

- The Conjunction "And"

- Possessive Suffixes

- Pronouns (subject, object, and pronominal suffixes)

- Adjectives (masculine, feminine, singular and plural)

- Prepositions (standalone, prefix, prefix with pronominal suffix)

- The Direct Object Marker, its suffixes, and attaching those suffixes directly to verbs

- Verbs (participles, past tense, future tense, reversing vav)

- Lots of great Biblical vocabulary, including proper names... and more!

Wow. **We know that our Lord is pleased, even more so because of your motives in learning His language: to understand His Word, to serve Him better, to love Him more.**

Let us thank Yeshua for His help in bringing us to this point in our studies.

Now, are you ready for some more good news? After the flashcards on the following pages, there will be only **one more lesson to study**. In that lesson, you will learn about two more verb forms: the *command* form (*imperative*) and the *infinitive*. Hang in there. Keep going. It's almost done. We know you can do it!

חֵטְא	בֹּקֶר
יִרְאָה	עֶרֶב
אוֹת	עֶזְרָה
ס.ל.ח	ח.ט.א
שׁ.ב.ת	ע.ז.ר

BŌ-ker
morning

noun, masculine, singular

(This word was introduced in Book 4, Lesson 6)

chayt
sin

noun, masculine, singular

(This word was introduced in Book 4, Lesson 6)

EH-rev
evening

noun, masculine, singular

(This word was introduced in Book 4, Lesson 6)

yir-AH
fear, awe

noun, feminine, singular

(This word was introduced in Book 4, Lesson 6)

ez-RAH
help

noun, feminine, singular

(This word was introduced in Book 4, Lesson 6)

ōt
sign

noun, common, singular

(This word was introduced in Book 4, Lesson 6)

sin

verb

(This word was introduced in Book 4, Lesson 6)

forgive

verb

(This word was introduced in Book 4, Lesson 6)

help

verb

(This word was introduced in Book 4, Lesson 6)

rest, cease
(i.e., cease from working)

verb

(This word was introduced in Book 4, Lesson 6)

Lesson 7:
Imperative And Infinitive Forms

This is the last lesson of this book, in which we will teach you the last two forms you need to know to complete your basic understanding of verbs: the *imperative* (command form) and the *infinitive*.

Before we show you these new verb forms, we want to present one final batch of Biblical vocabulary. The words in the following Word Lists appear frequently in the Bible and in the traditional prayers of Judaism. We hope you enjoy learning these words as much as we did!

Word List: Masculine Nouns

nations, peoples	*go-YIM*	mp	גּוֹיִם	nation, people*	*goy*	ms	גּוֹי
heads, chiefs	*rah-SHEEM*	mp	רָאשִׁים	head, chief*	*rōsh*	ms	רֹאשׁ

*Important notes about the words above:

The word *nation, people* גּוֹי is a synonym for a word you already know: עַם. Although the word גּוֹי is frequently used in scripture to refer to nations other than Israel (i.e., Gentiles), it is also used to refer to the nation or people of Israel (in at least 35 scriptural occurrences, by our count). The terms גּוֹי and עַם are even used interchangeably within the same verse to refer to the same group of people, as in Zephaniah 2:9, in which *both* terms are used to refer to the remnant of the nation of Israel. Note the emphasis on the last syllable of the plural form, which is based upon the Masoretic accent markings (although the majority of Jewish people today tend to put the emphasis on the first syllable during casual speech).

The word *head* רֹאשׁ is a versatile term which literally means that part of a person's or animal's body containing the brain, but figuratively means the "head" of a group: the *chief* item, the *principal* city, the *leader* of a nation, the *head* of a family, the *first* in a series (i.e., the *first* day of the month or year), the *highest* ranking priest or elder, the *top* of a mountain, the *source* of a river, the *choicest* gift. It can be used to *number* the people in Biblical census statistics: counting the *heads* of those who are battle ready; or *each*, as in how much tax should be paid *per person* or *per capita* (Latin *per capita* means "by head.")

Word List: Feminine Nouns

doorposts	*m'-zoo-ZŌT*	fp	מְזוּזֹת	doorpost*	*m'-zoo-ZAH*	fs	מְזוּזָה
troubles	*tsah-RŌT*	fp	צָרוֹת	trouble*	*tsah-RAH*	fs	צָרָה
years	*shah-NEEM*	fp	שָׁנִים	year*	*shah-NAH*	fs	שָׁנָה

*Important notes about the words above:

The word *doorpost* מְזוּזָה is a well-known word in Jewish culture. It literally means "a doorpost," but in modern Jewish life this word has come to also refer to the small decorative case containing a tiny scroll of scripture which is affixed to the doorpost of one's home in obedience to the commandment of Deut. 6:9 and 11:20, "You shall write [God's commandments] upon your doorposts and upon your gates."

The singular form of the word *trouble* צָרָה can also mean *distress*.

Note the masculine plural suffix for the word *year* שָׁנָה (even though this word is a feminine noun).

Word List: Verbs

bow, bend the knee	כ.ר.ע
forgive, pardon*	מ.ח.ל
rejoice	שׂ.מ.ח

*The verb *forgive* מ.ח.ל is a synonym for the verb you learned earlier, *forgive* ס.ל.ח, and... guess what? It, too, is always followed by the preposition *to/for* ל, just like ס.ל.ח!

new	חָדָשׁ, חֲדָשָׁה, חֲדָשִׁים, חֲדָשׁוֹת

The word *new* חָדָשׁ is an adjective, so it has four forms: masculine singular, feminine singular, masculine plural and feminine plural, shown above. This word can mean *new* as in "never-before-seen" or "brand new," or it can mean *renewed*. The phrase *B'rit Chadashah* used by Messianic believers to mean "New Testament" or "New Covenant" may be translated *renewed covenant* to express the concept that God has *renewed* His original covenant with Israel, but upon better terms: the sacrifice of Messiah Yeshua's blood. This *renewed* covenant extends to *any person* who chooses to receive His sacrificial gift in faith, just like the old one extended to anyone who wished to worship the God of Israel in faith.

Word List: Other Helpful Words

quickly	*m'-hay-RAH, bim-hay-RAH*	מְהֵרָה, בִּמְהֵרָה
faithful	*neh-eh-MAN*	נֶאֱמָן
awesome	*nō-RAH*	נוֹרָא
with*	*im*	עַם

*The word *with* עַם is another useful preposition, similar to the ones you learned earlier in our series. Like those other prepositions, it can have suffixes attached to it. For example, two common spellings found in scripture are *with us,* עִמָּנוּ and *with me,* עִמִּי

A Proper Noun

Rebecca	*riv-KAH*	רִבְקָה

You have learned the names *Abraham, Isaac,* and *Jacob; Sarah, Rachel* and *Leah.* The only person of all the famous patriarchs and matriarchs of Israel who we haven't taught yet in our series is *Rebecca.* We couldn't leave her out, of course! So here she is.

The Imperative In English

Okay! It's time to learn the *imperative* (command) form of Hebrew verbs. As per our usual method, we'll show you how the imperative works in English first. Let's think about how you would command someone to do something in English. For example, let's say you want to command your dog to stay on the lawn. You might say something like...

Fido, stay on the lawn!

You can see why this form is called the *imperative*. By *commanding* your dog, you have made it *imperative* that he obey.

What if you were watching over four children, two boys (John and Ben) and two girls (Sarah and Rachel). They want to play a game of catch outside, but they have a tendency to run out into the street to chase after the ball. Watching from the doorway, depending on which child or children you were commanding at the moment, you might holler any of the following sentences:

John, <u>stay</u> on the lawn!

John and Ben, <u>stay</u> on the lawn!

Sarah, <u>stay</u> on the lawn!

Sarah and Rachel, <u>stay</u> on the lawn!

Hey, you kids, <u>stay</u> on the lawn!

The great thing about the English imperative is that it doesn't change spelling, no matter who you are commanding. Boy, girl, plural, singular, animal, vegetable, mineral... it doesn't matter. In each situation, you just use the word "stay." Not so in Hebrew.

Hebrew Has Four Forms For The Imperative

The command form in Hebrew has four forms: **masculine singular, feminine singular, masculine plural and feminine plural.** This may remind you of the way that the participle has four forms. One interesting difference from the participle form, though, is that **the correct imperative form depends not on the person doing the commanding, but rather on the person (or persons) being commanded.** In other words, using our example of the four children, there would be four different forms in Hebrew for those commands, to address each of the four situations:

(1) commanding John (masculine singular)

(2) commanding John and Ben (masculine plural)

(3) commanding Sarah (feminine singular)

(4) commanding Sarah and Rachel (feminine plural)

The Imperative Is Formed From The "<u>You</u>" Future Tense

Thankfully, the Hebrew imperative forms come directly from certain future tense forms with slight changes. You already know the future tense, so you can apply your knowledge to help you recognize the imperative forms. **The Hebrew imperative forms are just slightly altered forms of the four "<u>you</u>" forms in the future tense.**

If you think about it, this totally makes sense. In English, we often get away with using the "<u>you</u>" future tense as a kind of command (though this is not the most pure usage of the future tense):

> John, <u>**you will stay**</u> on the lawn!
>
> John and Ben, <u>**you will stay**</u> on the lawn!
>
> Sarah, <u>**you will stay**</u> on the lawn!
>
> Sarah and Rachel, <u>**you will stay**</u> on the lawn!

In English, how do we create the *real* imperative form of a verb? We simply remove the subject and the helping verb from the future tense *(you will)*, and whatever remains is the true command form *(stay!)*. Hebrew uses a similar "paring down" process. Notice how the prefix *tahv* ת is stripped off the future tense (and other slight changes occur) to create the command form.

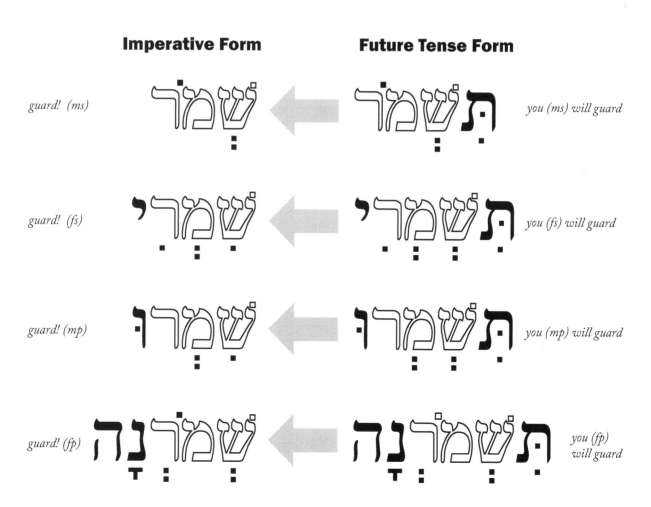

Imperative Form		**Future Tense Form**
guard! (ms)	שְׁמֹר ←	תִּשְׁמֹר *you (ms) will guard*
guard! (fs)	שִׁמְרִי ←	תִּשְׁמְרִי *you (fs) will guard*
guard! (mp)	שִׁמְרוּ ←	תִּשְׁמְרוּ *you (mp) will guard*
guard! (fp)	שְׁמֹרְנָה ←	תִּשְׁמֹרְנָה *you (fp) will guard*

Hebrew Has Two Patterns For The Imperative

Recall from Lesson 5 that the future tense actually has two spelling patterns. Many verbs follow the patterns having the *cholam* "ō" sound on the second syllable, such as the verb on the previous page. Other verbs follow the pattern which changes the vowel to the *patach* "ah" sound on the second syllable. The imperative form will follow whichever pattern the future tense uses for that particular verb. For example, the imperative of *hear* follows the same pattern as its future tense.

Imperative Form			**Future Tense Form**	
hear! (ms)	שְׁמַע	⬅	תִּשְׁמַע	*you (ms) will hear*
hear! (fs)	שִׁמְעִי	⬅	תִּשְׁמְעִי	*you (fs) will hear*
hear! (mp)	שִׁמְעוּ	⬅	תִּשְׁמְעוּ	*you (mp) will hear*
hear! (fp)	שְׁמַעְנָה	⬅	תִּשְׁמַעְנָה	*you (fp) will hear*

Scriptural Examples Of The Four Imperative Forms

Notice how the forms change depending on the gender and number of those being commanded.

וַיֹּאמֶר יהוה אֶל מֹשֶׁה כְּתֹב זֹאת זִכָּרוֹן בַּסֵּפֶר...

And the Lᴏʀᴅ said to Moses, **write** this [as a] memorial in the book...
God commands Moses (masculine singular), Exodus 17:14

אֶרֶץ, אֶרֶץ, אָרֶץ, שִׁמְעִי דְּבַר יהוה.

Land, land, land, **hear** the word of the Lᴏʀᴅ.
God commands the land (feminine singular), Jeremiah 22:29

...שִׁמְרוּ ...כָּל מִצְוֹת יהוה אֱלֹהֵיכֶם...

...**keep** all the commandments of the Lᴏʀᴅ your God...
David commands the leaders of Israel (masculine plural), 1 Chronicles 28:8

...שְׁמַעְנָה קוֹלִי, בָּנוֹת...

...**hear** my voice, daughters...
Isaiah commands the women of Jerusalem (feminine plural), Isaiah 32:9

The Imperative Form With Suffixes Attached

Recall from Lesson 2 that suffixes could be attached directly to verbs, in place of אֵת with a suffix. We called it "eliminating the middleman." We showed you a cartoon of a person writing books, and we showed you two sentences which both mean the same thing: "You wrote them." The first sentence uses the word אֵת with a suffix; the second one removes the middleman and attaches the suffix directly to the verb:

You wrote them.   כָּתַבְתָּ אוֹתָם.

You wrote them.   כְּתַבְתָּם.

The examples above use the past tense form, but, in the same way, we can attach suffixes directly to the imperative form. We're not going to ask you to learn to recognize all the varieties these forms can take, because the vowels change quite a bit. However, it is helpful to know the following examples which are frequently used in the prayers and songs of scripture (and in Judaism), in which the speaker is addressing the LORD.

redeem us   גְּאַל אוֹתָנוּ

                   גְּאָלֵנוּ

remember us   זְכֹר אוֹתָנוּ

                   זָכְרֵנוּ

An Irregular Imperative Form You Should Know

Of all the verbs you have worked with in past lessons, many of them have some pretty strange spellings when you put them in command form, so we won't even try to teach you all of those. One you should memorize, though, is the command form *do/make* in masculine singular.

Do! Make! (ms)   עֲשֵׂה!

We'll give you the chance to practice translating the imperative form straight from the scriptures in the next few pages, then we'll complete this lesson by teaching you the infinitive form.

Exercise 7.1 - Scripture Phrases

Translate each phrase into English. Each phrase contains at least one verb in the imperative form.

Jacob calls his sons together to prophesy over them (Genesis 49:2)

① הִקָּבְצוּ וְשִׁמְעוּ בְּנֵי יַעֲקֹב - וְשִׁמְעוּ אֶל יִשְׂרָאֵל אֲבִיכֶם.
assemble together

The words of the LORD, commanding Isaiah (Isaiah 62:11)

② ... אִמְרוּ לְבַת צִיּוֹן הִנֵּה יִשְׁעֵךְ בָּא ...
comes your salvation behold

God tells Moses to record Joshua's defeat of the Amalekites (Exodus 17:14)

③ וַיֹּאמֶר יהוה אֶל מֹשֶׁה כְּתֹב זֹאת זִכָּרוֹן בַּסֵּפֶר...
YHVH

After the locust swarms strip the land bare, Amos cries out for forgiveness (Amos 7:2)

④ וְהָיָה אִם כִּלָּה לֶאֱכוֹל אֶת עֵשֶׂב הָאָרֶץ וָאֹמַר אֲדֹנָי יהוה סְלַח נָא...
please   YHVH   grass of   of eating they finished when

God's warning to Israel and Judah to turn from evil and keep His commandments (2 Kings 17:13)

⑤ ... וְשִׁמְרוּ מִצְוֹתַי חֻקּוֹתַי כְּכָל הַתּוֹרָה אֲשֶׁר צִוִּיתִי אֶת אֲבֹתֵיכֶם ...
my statutes

Answers To Exercises On This Page

1. "Gather and hear, sons of Jacob – and listen to Israel your father."
2. "...Say to the daughter of Zion, 'Behold, your salvation comes...'"
3. And the LORD said to Moses, "Write this [as a] memorial in the book..."
4. And it came about when they had finished eating the grass of the land, I said, "Lord, LORD, forgive, please..."
5. "...and keep My commandments, My statutes, as [according to] all the Torah which I commanded your fathers..."

Exercise 7.1 - Scripture Phrases, *continued*

Moses reminds Israel to listen to God's commandments (Deuteronomy 6:4)

⑥ שְׁמַע, יִשְׂרָאֵל! יהוה אֱלֹהֵינוּ יהוה אֶחָד.

_____

Nathan's initial words of encouragement to King David to build the temple (2 Samuel 7:3)

⑦ וַיֹּאמֶר נָתָן אֶל הַמֶּלֶךְ, כֹּל אֲשֶׁר בִּלְבָבְךָ - לֵךְ, עֲשֵׂה, כִּי יהוה עִמָּךְ.
                                        go   *Nathan*

_____

Isaiah warns the women of Jerusalem of their coming tribulation (Isaiah 32:9)

⑧ נָשִׁים שַׁאֲנַנּוֹת, קֹמְנָה, שְׁמַעְנָה קוֹלִי! בָּנוֹת בֹּטְחוֹת, הַאְזֵנָּה אִמְרָתִי.
my speech   *give ear to*   *rise up*   *which are at ease*   *women*

_____

The prayer of Moses that God would spare His rebellious people (Deuteronomy 9:27)

⑨ זְכֹר לַעֲבָדֶיךָ לְאַבְרָהָם, לְיִצְחָק, וּלְיַעֲקֹב, אַל תֵּפֶן
                                             look   *not*

אֶל קְשִׁי הָעָם הַזֶּה, וְאֶל רִשְׁעוֹ, וְאֶל חַטָּאתוֹ.
                          its wickedness   *the stubborness of*

_____

The psalmist asks to be included in the salvation and favor God shows His people (Psalm 106:4)

⑩ זָכְרֵנִי יהוה, בִּרְצוֹן עַמֶּךְ - פָּקְדֵנִי בִּישׁוּעָתֶךָ.
           your salvation   *visit me*

_____

Answers To Exercises On This Page

6. Hear, Israel! The LORD our God, the LORD is one.

7. Nathan said to the king, "All that is in your heart – Go, do, for the LORD is with you."

8. Women who are at ease, get up, hear my voice! Trusting [complacent] daughters, give ear to my speech.

9. Remember your servants Abraham, Isaac and Jacob, and look not at the stubborness of this people, nor at their [its] wickedness, nor at their [its] sin.

10. Remember me, LORD, with [Your] favor of Your people – visit me with Your salvation.

_____

The Infinitive – Such A Simple Form!

You will love the simplicity of the infinitive. **The infinitive is a verb form which has no tense, no gender, and no number.** It doesn't get any simpler than that.

The Infinitive In English

In English, we form infinitives by adding the word "<u>to</u>" to our verbs:

to be **to rule** **to guard** **to go**

The infinitive has five different uses in the English language. It can transform a verb from its usual function into one of the following: *subject, direct object, subject complement, adjective*, or *adverb*. You don't need to memorize these five uses, but it would be very helpful to your Hebrew studies to be able to see them in action:

To go, after all that time, seemed like an afterthought.

"to go" is used as the subject of the sentence. "It" seemed like... "To go" seemed like...

We all really wanted **to go.**

"to go" is used as the direct object; it answers the question, "<u>What</u> did we want?"

My desire is **to go.**

"to go" acts a subject complement... similar to a direct object, except subject complements are used with linking verbs, such as "is."

I didn't have permission **to go.**

"to go" acts an adjective, which modifies the noun "permission," describing what <u>type</u> of permission the person is talking about.

He rented a car **to go** to Alaska.

"to go" acts an adverb, which modifies the verb "rented," describing <u>why</u> he rented a car.

The Infinitive In Hebrew

In Hebrew, too, the infinitive has many different uses. Some of those uses are the same as those in English. The Hebrew infinitive is most commonly formed by attaching a prefix *lahmed* ל to the verb's root letters and surrounding the letters with the vowel pattern shown:

If you think about it, this technique resembles our English method of placing a "to" in front of our verbs to create the infinitive. The prefix *lahmed* ל can mean "to" or "for" in Hebrew. Think of it as "to" when it is attached to a verb, and you will be able to easily recognize the infinitive form.

Examples Of The Infinitive In Hebrew

Applying the pattern for the infinitive to various verb root letters, we arrive at some fine examples of how the infinitive actually looks.

to remember	לִזְכֹּר
to find	לִמְצֹא
to guard	לִשְׁמֹר
to rule	לִמְלֹךְ

Unusual Forms Of The Infinitive

Certain verbs will have an additional *pah-tach* (ַ) vowel underneath the last consonant of their infinitive forms. Recall that, whenever this vowel appears under the *last* consonant of a word and that consonant is a *chayt* ח, *ah-yin* ע or dotted *hey* ה, you are dealing with a *furtive pah-tach*. In the case of the *chayt* or dotted *hey*, the syllable is pronounced *ach* חַ or *ah* הַ. Also, the syllable *before* the final syllable receives the emphasis on *all* words having a *furtive pah-tach*. Just mentally call upon the word *RU-ach* רוּחַ as an example to aid your pronunciation. We have included the transliterations on each unusual form below.

to trust	*liv-TŌ-ach*	לִבְטֹחַ
to hear	*lish-MŌ-ah*	לִשְׁמֹעַ
to forgive	*lis-LŌ-ach*	לִסְלֹחַ

Even More Unusual Forms Of The Infinitive

Certain verbs will have an additional *tahv* ת and will also lose a root letter or two as their infinitive is formed. There are many of these unusual forms, so we are listing the most prevalent ones you will see in scripture. To demonstrate how their root letters go "missing," we have listed their root forms to the right.

to give	לָתֵת	[נ.ת.ן]
to do / to make	לַעֲשׂוֹת	[ע.שׂ.ה]
to know	לָדַעַת	[י.ד.ע]

Examples Of The Infinitive In Scripture

חֶלְקִי יהוה, אָמַרְתִּי **לִשְׁמֹר** דְּבָרֶיךָ.

[You are] my portion, Lᴏʀᴅ, I have promised **to keep** your words. (Psalm 119:57)

...וְאֶת אֶלְעָזָר בְּנוֹ קִדְּשׁוּ **לִשְׁמֹר** אֶת אֲרוֹן יהוה.

...and Eleazar his son they consecrated **to guard** the ark of the Lᴏʀᴅ. (1 Sam. 7:1)

...וְהָיְתָה הַקֶּשֶׁת בֶּעָנָן – וּרְאִיתִיהָ **לִזְכֹּר** בְּרִית עוֹלָם...

The rainbow shall be in the cloud, and I will look on it **to remember** the everlasting covenant (Gen. 9:16)

...וְלֹא נָתַן יהוה לָכֶם לֵב **לָדַעַת**... וְאָזְנַיִם **לִשְׁמֹעַ**...

And the Lᴏʀᴅ has not given to you a heart **to know**... and ears **to hear**... (Deut. 29:4)

...וְשָׁמְרוּ דֶּרֶךְ יהוה, **לַעֲשׂוֹת** צְדָקָה...

...and they shall keep the way of the Lᴏʀᴅ, **to do** righteousness... (Gen. 18:19)

...וְנָתַן לְךָ אֶת כָּל הָאָרֶץ אֲשֶׁר דִּבֶּר **לָתֵת** לַאֲבֹתֶיךָ.

... and He will give you all the land that He promised **to give** to your fathers. (Deut. 19:8)

Infinitives To Express Obligation

In Hebrew, the infinitive may be teamed up with the preposition *upon* עַל in order to express obligation, such as "I ought" or "we must." This comes from the literal meaning of "upon" in the sense of an obligation resting "upon" someone. The sentences below illustrate.

It is upon me to keep the commandment.
or I must keep the commandment.
or I ought to keep the commandment.

עָלַי לִשְׁמֹר אֶת הַמִּצְוָה.

...it is upon us to do.
or ...we must do.
or ...it is our duty to do.

...עָלֵינוּ לַעֲשׂוֹת. (from Ezra 10:12)

Infinitives Following The Verb *Give* נ.ת.ן

Certain phrases in Hebrew don't translate well literally, and one example is when infinitives follow the verb *give* נ.ת.ן. Most times in this situation, you'll want to translate it as *enable*, *permit* or *allow*, rather than the literal meaning of *give*. The infinitive doesn't have to follow directly after the verb *give* נ.ת.ן, though; there may be other words inserted between the two verbs.

יֵשׁוּעַ נָתַן לָנוּ לָדַעַת אֶת הָאָב.

Yeshua has allowed us to know the Father.
or Yeshua has enabled us to know the Father.

A Special Infinitive: *To Say* לֵאמֹר

The infinitive of the verb *say* א.מ.ר is spelled לֵאמֹר and appears more than 930 times in the Hebrew scriptures! Although it technically means "to say," the majority of the times it is used in scripture it is best to translate it "saying." It just makes the English sound a little less awkward. The most famous phrases throughout scripture which use this infinitive are:

דַּבֵּר אֶל בְּנֵי יִשְׂרָאֵל, לֵאמֹר...

Speak to the sons of Israel, saying...

וַיֹּאמֶר מֹשֶׁה אֶל בְּנֵי יִשְׂרָאֵל, לֵאמֹר...

Moses said to the children of Israel, saying...

Infinitives With Other Prepositions Attached

We have learned that most infinitives are formed by attaching the prefix לְ. Conveniently, that prepositional prefix means *to*, so it works out just fine for infinitives. But, did you know that *other* prepositional prefixes can become attached to an infinitive, *instead* of the letter לְ? Occasionally, you'll come across an infinitive with a בְּ or a כְּ attached. If you see this, you can just translate the prefix part of the verb as *while* or *when*.

If you think about this, it does kind of make sense. If the prefix לְ causes us to translate a verb "<u>to</u> guard," for example, then the prefix בְּ might cause us to say "<u>in</u> guarding." Likewise, the prefix כְּ usually has the meaning "as," so we might translate the verb "<u>as</u> he guarded." These are not, of course, *truly* literal translations of the infinitive, but they are the best we can do in English without using incorrect syntax. That's why we suggested using the terms *while* or *when* in your translations. Scriptural examples:

וַיְהִי, בִּשְׁמוֹר יוֹאָב אֶל הָעִיר...

And it came to pass, **in guarding** the city, Joab...
or And it came to pass, **while** Joab **guarded** the city...
(from 2 Samuel 11:16)

וַיְהִי, כִּשְׁמוֹעַ הַמֶּלֶךְ אֶת דְּבַר אִישׁ הָאֱלֹהִים...

And it came to pass, **as** the king **heard** the word of the man of God...
or And it came to pass, **when** the king **heard** the word of the man of God...
(from 1 Kings 13:4)

Infinitives Can Take Suffixes, Too

One last little thing to be aware of... infinitives can also take suffixes. The suffixes are fairly similar to the possessive endings which are attached to nouns. Here are some scriptural examples.

וַיִּשְׁלַח שָׁאוּל מַלְאָכִים אֶל בֵּית דָּוִד לְשָׁמְרוֹ...

Saul sent messengers to the house of David **to watch him**...
(from 1 Samuel 19:11)

כִּי מַלְאָכָיו יְצַוֶּה לָּךְ לְשָׁמְרְךָ בְּכָל דְּרָכֶיךָ.

For He will command His angels concerning you, **to guard you** in all your ways.
(Psalm 91:11)

Exercise 7.2 - Scripture Phrases

Translate each phrase into English. Each phrase contains at least one verb in the infinitive form.

The LORD formalizes His covenant promise to Abram (Genesis 15:18)

① ...כָּרַת יְהוָה אֶת אַבְרָם בְּרִית, לֵאמֹר, לְזַרְעֲךָ נָתַתִּי אֶת הָאָרֶץ הַזֹּאת....

cut   *YHVH*   *Abram*

The entire world seeks an audience with Solomon (1 Kings 10:24)

② וְכָל הָאָרֶץ מְבַקְשִׁים אֶת פְּנֵי שְׁלֹמֹה לִשְׁמֹעַ אֶת חָכְמָתוֹ, אֲשֶׁר נָתַן אֱלֹהִים בְּלִבּוֹ.

seeking   *Solomon*   *his wisdom*

Moses reiterates the Torah to all the people (Deuteronomy 15:5)

③ ...תִּשְׁמַע בְּקוֹל יְהוָה אֱלֹהֶיךָ, לִשְׁמֹר לַעֲשׂוֹת אֶת כָּל הַמִּצְוָה הַזֹּאת...

YHVH

After Adam and Eve eat the fruit, God banishes them from Eden (Genesis 3:22)

④ וַיֹּאמֶר יְהוָה אֱלֹהִים, הֵן, הָאָדָם הָיָה כְּאַחַד מִמֶּנּוּ, לָדַעַת טוֹב וָרָע...

behold   *the man*   *like one*

Joshua's spies promise Rahab protection in return for her help (Joshua 2:14)

⑤ ...וְהָיָה, בְּתֵת יהוה לָנוּ אֶת הָאָרֶץ, וְעָשִׂינוּ עִמָּךְ חֶסֶד וָאֱמֶת.

Answers 7.2 - Scripture Phrases

1. ...the LORD made a covenant with Abram, saying, "To your seed I have given this land..."
   Literal translation: *YHVH cut a covenant with Abram, to say, "To your seed I have given this land..."*

2. And all the earth sought the presence of Solomon to hear his wisdom, which God had put in his heart.
   Literal translation: *And all the earth seeking the face of Solomon to hear the wisdom which God had given in his heart.*

3. You will listen to the voice of the LORD your God, to observe to do all these commandments...
   Literal translation: *You will listen to the voice of YHVH your God, to observe to do all this commandment...*

4. And the LORD said, "Behold, the man has become like one of Us, to know good and evil..."

5. And it shall come to pass, when the LORD gives us the land, we will deal with you kindly and faithfully...
   Literal translation: *And it shall be, in the LORD's giving us the land, we will do to you kindness and truth.*

A Complete Verb Pattern

Congratulations! You have learned ALL the forms of the Hebrew verb. Let's review all the forms you know.

- **participle**
- **past tense**
- **future tense**
- **imperative (command)**
- **infinitive**

Wow. That's fantastic! Just look at how many tools of knowledge you have at your disposal.

We bet you are thinking, "I wish I had had the presence of mind to write down all the forms of these verbs on one sheet of paper while I was studying them." We have good news for you. You don't need to reinvent the wheel. The thing you are wishing for has already been invented, and it is called a **verb chart** (or a **verb table**). Verb charts have been around ever since people began studying foreign languages (probably since the tower of Babel debacle).

An Example Of A Verb Chart

Check out this handy-dandy chart. It's like having a nice toolbox with compartments for organizing all your tools. You will love it! The example below is for the verb *remember*, ז.כ.ר.

Imperative		Future		Past		ז.כ.ר *remember*
זְכֹר	*ms*	אֶזְכֹּר	*1cs*	זָכַרְתִּי	*1cs*	
זִכְרִי	*fs*	תִּזְכֹּר	*2ms*	זָכַרְתָּ	*2ms*	
זִכְרוּ	*mp*	תִּזְכְּרִי	*2fs*	זָכַרְתְּ	*2fs*	**Infinitive** לִזְכֹּר
זְכֹרְנָה	*fp*	יִזְכֹּר	*3ms*	זָכַר	*3ms*	
		תִּזְכֹּר	*3fs*	זָכְרָה	*3fs*	**Present/ Participle**
		נִזְכֹּר	*1cp*	זָכַרְנוּ	*1cp*	זוֹכֵר *ms*
		תִּזְכְּרוּ	*2mp*	זְכַרְתֶּם	*2mp*	זוֹכֶרֶת *fs*
		תִּזְכֹּרְנָה	*2fp*	זְכַרְתֶּן	*2fp*	זוֹכְרִים *mp*
		יִזְכְּרוּ	*3mp*	זָכְרוּ	*3cp*	זוֹכְרוֹת *fp*
		תִּזְכֹּרְנָה	*3fp*			

*The symbol < above a syllable indicates that syllable is stressed (receives emphasis). If there is no < , then stress the last syllable.

More Verb Charts At The End Of This Book

At the end of this book (in the pages just before the Glossary), you will find verb charts for the most frequently used verbs we have taught you in the *Messiah's Alphabet* series. You can refer to these charts to confirm the tenses of these verbs as you come across them in scripture.

What About Other Verb Patterns?

The pattern we taught you in this book (the one shown in the verb chart on the previous page) is the most common Hebrew pattern by far. It is called the *pah-ahl* פָּעַל pattern. However, this is only one of *seven* complete patterns that exist for Hebrew verbs. The other six are used for specific situations – things like the passive or reflexive voice, or the causative or intensive moods. As we said, you are not as likely to come across these specific situations, so we focused on teaching you the most frequently used pattern. Get this pattern under your belt now, and if you decide to pursue Biblical Hebrew in greater depth later on, you will be able to tackle the other six patterns.

Where To Go From Here

You have built a fine foundation in basic Hebrew grammar – enough to study a good bit of the scriptures – provided that you have access to an interlinear Bible or Bible software with Strong's numbers so that you can hunt down the definitions of any unfamiliar words you come across. In the past, we advised that you acquire a copy of Hendrickson's *Interlinear Bible* and *Strong's Concordance with Hebrew and Greek Lexicon*. If you already own these books, fantastic. They are the first step to figure out the basic meaning of a Hebrew word in scripture. If you're not a hardcopy kind of person, then most Bible software programs (installed versions, website versions, free apps, etc.) usually incorporate these two books directly into their programs, making them electronically searchable (and that's a real time saver).

As wonderful as those two publications may be, you have reached the point in your studies that they can no longer answer all your questions. Now you know that **prefixes, suffixes and verb forms make a <u>huge</u> difference to the meaning of a word.** Strong's Lexicon cannot take you to that level of understanding, and it's not intended to. What you need now is a book that can describe what each word's gender, person and number are, or what its pronominal suffix means, or whether a prefix is conjunctive, reversing, or prepositional, or what tense is represented by a certain verb form. This kind of detailed analysis is called *parsing*. There is a four-volume set we turn to regularly when we need to parse the scriptures, called the *Analytical Key to the Old Testament* by John Joseph Owens. If you would like to have *all* the grammatical information about *every* word of the Hebrew scriptures at your fingertips, we highly recommend owning a copy. (Frankly, we ourselves cannot do without it.)

In addition, please rest assured that it is our goal to write many more workbooks that will provide lots of guided practice in reading the Hebrew scriptures. It's our hope that we will *never* stop adding to the *Messiah's Alphabet* series, so that you may have ongoing opportunities to explore the depths of Biblical Hebrew and related studies. Every now and then, take a moment to visit your favorite online book retailers to look for newly released books in the *Messiah's Alphabet* series. We hope to write many more in the years to come.

Congratulations!

Congratulations! You have completed Book 4 of the *Messiah's Alphabet* series!

We are amazed and delighted that you were able to complete your Hebrew studies up to this point. Each time you complete a book like this, it represents a series of miraculous triumphs in your life, accomplished by God's grace through the power of the Holy Spirit against the forces of the world, the flesh, and the devil. We are well aware of the spiritual opposition you have experienced while you were studying this book as an act of dedication to God's Word. We ourselves have experienced the same thing; we know what it takes to persevere through all the trials, and we are exceptionally proud of you.

Now, press on. "Fight the good fight of the faith. Take hold of the eternal life to which you were called when you made your good confession in the presence of many witnesses" (1 Timothy 6:12). What area of service has He called you to next? Our prayer for you is that you succeed mightily, whether it be in Biblical language study or in a completely different area of ministry.

Let us make this a moment of remembrance – a *zikaron* זִכָּרוֹן – as we say a blessing together:

Blessed are You, Lord our God, King of the Universe, Who has given me the grace, perseverance and understanding to study Your Biblical language. Thank You for the joy You have brought me through this study. May I bless Your Name by not only hearing, but doing, as I am commanded in Your Word.

We're going to close this lesson with your vocabulary flashcards as usual. Immediately following the flashcard pages you will find:

- **a list of our other books**
- **verb charts of the most frequently used verbs you have learned**
- **a glossary of the lexical forms of all words you have learned in this series**

It's our goal to write more workbooks for Biblical Hebrew and related studies as our Lord permits. Be on the lookout for future books in the *Messiah's Alphabet* series, available through online book retailers.

רֹאשׁ	גּוֹי
צָרָה	מְזוּזָה
חָדָשׁ חֲדָשָׁה, חֲדָשִׁים, חֲדָשׁוֹת	שָׁנָה
נֶאֱמָן	מְהֵרָה, בִּמְהֵרָה
רִבְקָה	נוֹרָא

goy
nation, people

noun, masculine, singular

(This word was introduced in Book 4, Lesson 7)

rōsh
head, chief

noun, masculine, singular

(This word was introduced in Book 4, Lesson 7)

m'-zoo-ZAH
doorpost

noun, feminine, singular

(This word was introduced in Book 4, Lesson 7)

tsah-RAH
trouble

noun, feminine, singular

(This word was introduced in Book 4, Lesson 7)

shah-NAH
year

noun, feminine, singular

(This word was introduced in Book 4, Lesson 7)

chah-DAHSH
new, adjective

chah-dah-SHAH, chah-dah-SHEEM, chah-dah-SHÔT

(This word was introduced in Book 4, Lesson 7)

m'-hay-RAH, bim-hay-RAH
quickly

(This word was introduced in Book 4, Lesson 7)

neh-eh-MAHN
faithful

(This word was introduced in Book 4, Lesson 7)

nō-RAH
awesome

(This word was introduced in Book 4, Lesson 7)

riv-KAH
Rebecca

proper noun

(This word was introduced in Book 4, Lesson 7)

כ.ר.ע	עִם
שׂ.מ.ח	מ.ח.ל

Jim and Lisa triumphantly announce their completion of "Messiah's Alphabet Book 4"

with

preposition

(This word was introduced in Book 4, Lesson 7)

bow, bend the knee

verb

(This word was introduced in Book 4, Lesson 7)

forgive, pardon

verb

(This word was introduced in Book 4, Lesson 7)

rejoice

verb

(This word was introduced in Book 4, Lesson 7)

"Dear reader:
We're so proud of you for completing your
studies in Hebrew to this level!"
- Jim and Lisa

Other Books
by James T. and Lisa M. Cummins

Messiah's Alphabet: Names Have Meaning is an exploration into the actual Hebrew meanings of the names of certain people mentioned in the Bible. Surprising discoveries will unfold as you connect the true meaning of each Hebrew name with its prophetic significance and fulfillment in scripture. The hidden Hebrew meanings underlying the names of New Testament people and places will also be brought to light. While a basic knowledge of the Hebrew and Greek alphabets may be helpful, it is not necessary, as all pronunciations are provided in transliteration form using the standard alphabet of English. All answers are provided in the text. Audio files of every lesson available.

Available now through online book retailers

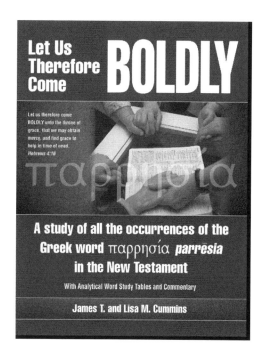

Let Us Therefore Come BOLDLY: A study of all the occurrences of the Greek word parresia *in the New Testament*

This book leads the reader through all the occurrences of the Greek word for "boldness" in the New Testament. Throughout the study, the various meanings of this deep and wonderful Greek word are uncovered, along with practical applications for the believer's life. Graphic tables and insightful commentary make it easy for the student to understand the significance of every separate mention of the Greek word *parresia* – even if the student has no knowledge of the Greek language.

Available now through online book retailers

Other Books by James T. and Lisa M. Cummins, *continued*

Phrase-By-Phrase Harmony of the Gospels – This is a visual, side-by-side arrangement of every phrase of the books of Matthew, Mark, Luke and John, in chronological order. Every phrase of every gospel is aligned side by side with the corresponding phrases in the other gospels, in table format. Each event includes its own geographical map and graphical timeline. Blended narrative contains every fact and detail of all four gospels, merged into a single, readable, chronological account.

Available now through online book retailers

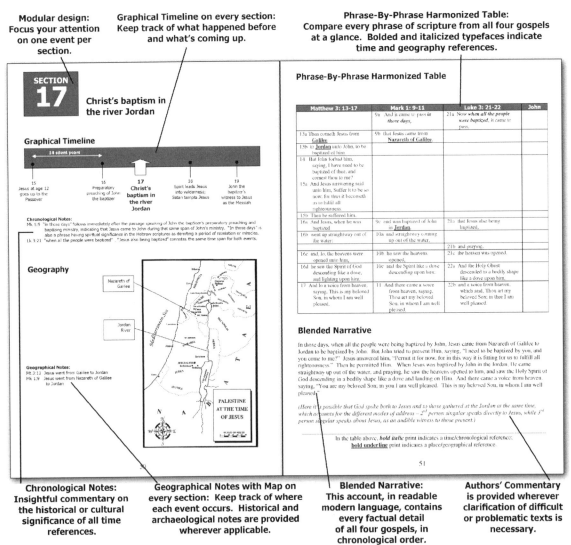

Modular design: Focus your attention on one event per section.

Graphical Timeline on every section: Keep track of what happened before and what's coming up.

Phrase-By-Phrase Harmonized Table: Compare every phrase of scripture from all four gospels at a glance. Bolded and italicized typefaces indicate time and geography references.

Chronological Notes: Insightful commentary on the historical or cultural significance of all time references.

Geographical Notes with Map on every section: Keep track of where each event occurs. Historical and archaeological notes are provided wherever applicable.

Blended Narrative: This account, in readable modern language, contains every factual detail of all four gospels, in chronological order.

Authors' Commentary is provided wherever clarification of difficult or problematic texts is necessary.

Other Books by James T. and Lisa M. Cummins, *continued*

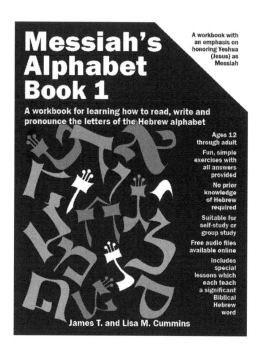

Messiah's Alphabet Book 1: A workbook for learning how to read, write and pronounce the letters of the Hebrew alphabet
The first book in the *Messiah's Alphabet* series introduces the Hebrew alphabet to those with no prior knowledge of Hebrew. The student is shown how to draw simple "stick figure" shapes for each letter, and then learns the sound and name of each letter in a fun and friendly manner. The book gradually introduces some of the most frequently used Hebrew words in the Bible, gently assisting the reader in learning to recognize and pronounce each one. Audio files of every lesson available.

Available now through online book retailers

Messiah's Alphabet Book 2:
Building a Biblical Vocabulary
The second book in the *Messiah's Alphabet* series, this workbook teaches basic Hebrew grammar on topics such as the definite article "the", the conjunction "and," plural nouns, adjectives and possessives for singular nouns. Guided readings of short scripture passages are included throughout. Fun, simple exercises with all answers are provided. Puzzles, riddles and tear-out "flashcard" pages are included. Intended for students who have completed Book 1 or who have a solid working knowledge of the Hebrew alphabet and are able to phonetically "sound out" Hebrew words. Audio files of every lesson available.

Available now through online book retailers

Other Books by James T. and Lisa M. Cummins, *continued*

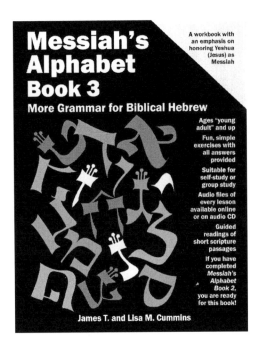

Messiah's Alphabet Book 3: More Grammar For Biblical Hebrew

The third book in the *Messiah's Alphabet* series covers topics such as participles, prepositions (standalone and inseparable), prepositions with pronominal suffixes, and construct chains (word pairs). Each lesson introduces plenty of new Biblical Hebrew vocabulary. Continuing in the same fun and friendly style as the other books in the series, the workbook contains cartoons, jokes, puzzles, flashcard pages, and answers to all exercises. Audio files of every lesson available.

Available now through online book retailers

Verb Charts

Imperative		Future		Past		א.ה.ב
אֱהַב	ms	אֹהַב	1cs	אָהַ֫בְתִּי	1cs	*love*
אֶהֲבִי	fs	תֹּאהַב	2ms	אָהַ֫בְתָּ	2ms	
אֶהֲבוּ	mp	תֹּאהֲבִי	2fs	אָהַבְתְּ	2fs	**Infinitive**
אֱהֹ֫בְנָה	fp	יֹאהַב	3ms	אָהַב	3ms	לֶאֱהֹב
		תֹּאהַב	3fs	אָהֲבָה	3fs	**Present/ Participle**
		נֹאהַב	1cp	אָהַ֫בְנוּ	1cp	אוֹהֵב ms
		תֹּאהֲבוּ	2mp	אֲהַבְתֶּם	2mp	אוֹהֶ֫בֶת fs
		תֹּאהֹ֫בְנָה	2fp	אֲהַבְתֶּן	2fp	אוֹהֲבִים mp
		יֹאהֲבוּ	3mp	אָהֲבוּ	3cp	אוֹהֲבוֹת fp
		תֹּאהֹ֫בְנָה	3fp			

Imperative		Future		Past		א.מ.ר
אֱמֹר	ms	אֹמַר	1cs	אָמַ֫רְתִּי	1cs	*say*
אִמְרִי	fs	תֹּאמַר	2ms	אָמַ֫רְתָּ	2ms	
אִמְרוּ	mp	תֹּאמְרִי	2fs	אָמַרְתְּ	2fs	**Infinitive***
אֱמֹ֫רְנָה	fp	יֹאמַר	3ms	אָמַר	3ms	לֵמוֹר
		תֹּאמַר	3fs	אָמְרָה	3fs	**Present/ Participle**
		נֹאמַר	1cp	אָמַ֫רְנוּ	1cp	אוֹמֵר ms
		תֹּאמְרוּ	2mp	אֲמַרְתֶּם	2mp	אוֹמֶ֫רֶת fs
		תֹּאמַ֫רְנָה	2fp	אֲמַרְתֶּן	2fp	אוֹמְרִים mp
		יֹאמְרוּ	3mp	אָמְרוּ	3cp	אוֹמְרוֹת fp
		תֹּאמַ֫רְנָה	3fp			

*The Biblical (archaic) spelling of the infinitive is shown in this chart. Its modern Hebrew spelling is לוֹמַר.

Verb Charts, *continued*

Imperative		Future		Past		ב.ח.ר *choose*
בְּחַר	ms	אֶבְחַר	1cs	בָּחַרְתִּי	1cs	
בַּחֲרִי	fs	תִּבְחַר	2ms	בָּחַרְתָּ	2ms	
בַּחֲרוּ	mp	תִּבְחֲרִי	2fs	בָּחַרְתְּ	2fs	**Infinitive**
בְּחַרְנָה	fp	יִבְחַר	3ms	בָּחַר	3ms	לִבְחֹר
		תִּבְחַר	3fs	בָּחֲרָה	3fs	
		נִבְחַר	1cp	בָּחַרְנוּ	1cp	**Present/ Participle**
		תִּבְחֲרוּ	2mp	בְּחַרְתֶּם	2mp	בּוֹחֵר	ms
		תִּבְחַרְנָה	2fp	בְּחַרְתֶּן	2fp	בּוֹחֶרֶת	fs
		יִבְחֲרוּ	3mp	בָּחֲרוּ	3cp	בּוֹחֲרִים	mp
		תִּבְחַרְנָה	3fp			בּוֹחֲרוֹת	fp

Imperative		Future		Past		ב.ט.ח *trust*
בְּטַח	ms	אֶבְטַח	1cs	בָּטַֽחְתִּי	1cs	
בִּטְחִי	fs	תִּבְטַח	2ms	בָּטַֽחְתָּ	2ms	
בִּטְחוּ	mp	תִּבְטְחִי	2fs	בָּטַחַתְּ	2fs	**Infinitive**
בְּטַחְנָה	fp	יִבְטַח	3ms	בָּטַח	3ms	לִבְטֹחַ
		תִּבְטַח	3fs	בָּטְחָה	3fs	
		נִבְטַח	1cp	בָּטַֽחְנוּ	1cp	**Present/ Participle**
		תִּבְטְחוּ	2mp	בְּטַחְתֶּם	2mp	בּוֹטֵֽחַ	ms
		תִּבְטַֽחְנָה	2fp	בְּטַחְתֶּן	2fp	בּוֹטַֽחַת	fs
		יִבְטְחוּ	3mp	בָּטְחוּ	3cp	בּוֹטְחִים	mp
		תִּבְטַֽחְנָה	3fp			בּוֹטְחוֹת	fp

Verb Charts, *continued*

Imperative		Future		Past		ג.א.ל
גְּאַל	ms	אֶגְאַל	1cs	גָּאַ֫לְתִּי	1cs	*redeem, rescue*
גַּאֲלִי	fs	תִּגְאַל	2ms	גָּאַ֫לְתָּ	2ms	
גַּאֲלוּ	mp	תִּגְאֲלִי	2fs	גָּאַלְתְּ	2fs	Infinitive
גְּאַ֫לְנָה	fp	יִגְאַל	3ms	גָּאַל	3ms	לִגְאַל
		תִּגְאַל	3fs	גָּאֲלָה	3fs	Present/ Participle
		נִגְאַל	1cp	גָּאַ֫לְנוּ	1cp	גּוֹאֵל ms
		תִּגְאֲלוּ	2mp	גְּאַלְתֶּם	2mp	גּוֹאֶ֫לֶת fs
		תִּגְאַ֫לְנָה	2fp	גְּאַלְתֶּן	2fp	גּוֹאֲלִים mp
		יִגְאֲלוּ	3mp	גָּאֲלוּ	3cp	גּוֹאֲלוֹת fp
		תִּגְאַ֫לְנָה	3fp			

Imperative		Future		Past		ה.י.ה
הֱיֵה	ms	אֶהְיֶה	1cs	הָיִ֫יתִי	1cs	*be, exist*
הֱיִי	fs	תִּהְיֶה	2ms	הָיִ֫יתָ	2ms	
הֱיוּ	mp	תִּהְיִי	2fs	הָיִית	2fs	Infinitive
הֱיֶ֫ינָה	fp	יִהְיֶה	3ms	הָיָה	3ms	לִהְיוֹת
		תִּהְיֶה	3fs	הָיְתָה	3fs	Present/ Participle
		נִהְיֶה	1cp	הָיִ֫ינוּ	1cp	הוֹיֶה ms
		תִּהְיוּ	2mp	הֱיִיתֶם	2mp	הוֹיָה fs
		תִּהְיֶ֫ינָה	2fp	הֱיִיתֶן	2fp	הוֹיִים mp
		יִהְיוּ	3mp	הָיוּ	3cp	הוֹיוֹת fp
		תִּהְיֶ֫ינָה	3fp			

Verb Charts, *continued*

Imperative		Future		Past		הָלַךְ **ה.ל.ךְ**
לֵךְ	ms	אֵלֵךְ	1cs	הָלַכְתִּי	1cs	*walk, go*
לְכִי	fs	תֵּלֵךְ	2ms	הָלַכְתָּ	2ms	
לְכוּ	mp	תֵּלְכִי	2fs	הָלַכְתְּ	2fs	**Infinitive**
לֵכְנָה	fp	יֵלֵךְ	3ms*	הָלַךְ	3ms	לָלֶכֶת
		תֵּלֵךְ	3fs	הָלְכָה	3fs	**Present/ Participle**
		נֵלֵךְ	1cp	הָלַכְנוּ	1cp	הוֹלֵךְ ms
		תֵּלְכוּ	2mp	הֲלַכְתֶּם	2mp	הוֹלֶכֶת fs
		תֵּלַכְנָה	2fp	הֲלַכְתֶּן	2fp	הוֹלְכִים mp
*A rarely used alternate form of this word is spelled יַהֲלֹךְ.		יֵלְכוּ	3mp	הָלְכוּ	3cp	הוֹלְכוֹת fp
		תֵּלַכְנָה	3fp			

Imperative		Future		Past		זָכַר **ז.כ.ר**
זְכֹר	ms	אֶזְכֹּר	1cs	זָכַרְתִּי	1cs	*remember*
זִכְרִי	fs	תִּזְכֹּר	2ms	זָכַרְתָּ	2ms	
זִכְרוּ	mp	תִּזְכְּרִי	2fs	זָכַרְתְּ	2fs	**Infinitive**
זְכֹרְנָה	fp	יִזְכֹּר	3ms	זָכַר	3ms	לִזְכֹּר
		תִּזְכֹּר	3fs	זָכְרָה	3fs	**Present/ Participle**
		נִזְכֹּר	1cp	זָכַרְנוּ	1cp	זוֹכֵר ms
		תִּזְכְּרוּ	2mp	זְכַרְתֶּם	2mp	זוֹכֶרֶת fs
		תִּזְכֹּרְנָה	2fp	זְכַרְתֶּן	2fp	זוֹכְרִים mp
		יִזְכְּרוּ	3mp	זָכְרוּ	3cp	זוֹכְרוֹת fp
		תִּזְכֹּרְנָה	3fp			

Verb Charts, *continued*

ח.ט.א — sin

Imperative		Future		Past	
חֲטָא	ms	אֶחֱטָא	1cs	חָטָ֫אתִי	1cs
חִטְאִי	fs	תֶּחֱטָא	2ms	חָטָ֫אתָ	2ms
חִטְאוּ	mp	תֶּחֶטְאִי	2fs	חָטָאת	2fs
חֲטֶ֫אנָה	fp	יֶחֱטָא	3ms	חָטָא	3ms
		תֶּחֱטָא	3fs	חָטְאָה	3fs
		נֶחֱטָא	1cp	חָטָ֫אנוּ	1cp
		תֶּחֶטְאוּ	2mp	חֲטָאתֶם	2mp
		תֶּחֱטֶ֫אנָה	2fp	חֲטָאתֶן	2fp
		יֶחֶטְאוּ	3mp	חָטְאוּ	3cp
		תֶּחֱטֶ֫אנָה	3fp		

Infinitive

לַחֲטֹא

Present/Participle

חוֹטֵא	ms
חוֹטֵאת	fs
חוֹטְאִים	mp
חוֹטְאוֹת	fp

י.ד.ע — know

Imperative		Future		Past	
דַּע	ms	אֵדַע	1cs	יָדַ֫עְתִּי	1cs
דְּעִי	fs	תֵּדַע	2ms	יָדַ֫עְתָּ	2ms
דְּעוּ	mp	תֵּדְעִי	2fs	יָדַ֫עַתְּ	2fs
דַּ֫עְנָה	fp	יֵדַע	3ms	יָדַע	3ms
		תֵּדַע	3fs	יָדְעָה	3fs
		נֵדַע	1cp	יָדַ֫עְנוּ	1cp
		תֵּדְעוּ	2mp	יְדַעְתֶּם	2mp
		תֵּדַ֫עְנָה	2fp	יְדַעְתֶּן	2fp
		יֵדְעוּ	3mp	יָדְעוּ	3cp
		תֵּדַ֫עְנָה	3fp		

Infinitive*

לָדַעַת

Present/Participle

יוֹדֵעַ	ms
יוֹדַעַת	fs
יוֹדְעִים	mp
יוֹדְעוֹת	fp

*An alternate spelling of the infinitive form is לֵדַע.

Verb Charts, *continued*

Imperative		Future		Past		י.שׁ.ב
שֵׁב	*ms*	אֵשֵׁב	*1cs*	יָשַׁבְתִּי	*1cs*	*sit, dwell*
שְׁבִי	*fs*	תֵּשֵׁב	*2ms*	יָשַׁבְתָּ	*2ms*	
שְׁבוּ	*mp*	תֵּשְׁבִי	*2fs*	יָשַׁבְתְּ	*2fs*	**Infinitive***
שֵׁבְנָה	*fp*	יֵשֵׁב	*3ms*	יָשַׁב	*3ms*	לָשֶׁבֶת
		תֵּשֵׁב	*3fs*	יָשְׁבָה	*3fs*	**Present/ Participle**
		נֵשֵׁב	*1cp*	יָשַׁבְנוּ	*1cp*	יוֹשֵׁב *ms*
		תֵּשְׁבוּ	*2mp*	יְשַׁבְתֶּם	*2mp*	יוֹשֶׁבֶת *fs*
		תֵּשַׁבְנָה	*2fp*	יְשַׁבְתֶּן	*2fp*	יוֹשְׁבִים *mp*
A modern, alternate form of the infinitive is לֵשֵׁב.		יֵשְׁבוּ	*3mp*	יָשְׁבוּ	*3cp*	יוֹשְׁבוֹת *fp*
		תֵּשַׁבְנָה	*3fp*			

Imperative		Future		Past		כ.ר.ע
כְּרַע	*ms*	אֶכְרַע	*1cs*	כָּרַעְתִּי	*1cs*	*kneel, bow down*
כִּרְעִי	*fs*	תִּכְרַע	*2ms*	כָּרַעְתָּ	*2ms*	
כִּרְעוּ	*mp*	תִּכְרְעִי	*2fs*	כָּרַעְתְּ	*2fs*	**Infinitive**
כְּרַעְנָה	*fp*	יִכְרַע	*3ms*	כָּרַע	*3ms*	לִכְרֹעַ
		תִּכְרַע	*3fs*	כָּרְעָה	*3fs*	**Present/ Participle**
		נִכְרַע	*1cp*	כָּרַעְנוּ	*1cp*	כּוֹרֵעַ *ms*
		תִּכְרְעוּ	*2mp*	כְּרַעְתֶּם	*2mp*	כּוֹרַעַת *fs*
		תִּכְרַעְנָה	*2fp*	כְּרַעְתֶּן	*2fp*	כּוֹרְעִים *mp*
		יִכְרְעוּ	*3mp*	כָּרְעוּ	*3cp*	כּוֹרְעוֹת *fp*
		תִּכְרַעְנָה	*3fp*			

Verb Charts, *continued*

Imperative			Future			Past				
									כ.ת.ב	
									write	
כְּתֹב	*ms*		אֶכְתֹּב	*1cs*		כָּתַֿבְתִּי	*1cs*			
כִּתְבִי	*fs*		תִּכְתֹּב	*2ms*		כָּתַֿבְתָּ	*2ms*		**Infinitive**	
כִּתְבוּ	*mp*		תִּכְתְּבִי	*2fs*		כָּתַבְתְּ	*2fs*		לִכְתֹּב	
כְּתֹֿבְנָה	*fp*		יִכְתֹּב	*3ms*		כָּתַב	*3ms*			
			תִּכְתֹּב	*3fs*		כָּתְבָה	*3fs*		**Present/ Participle**	
			נִכְתֹּב	*1cp*		כָּתַֿבְנוּ	*1cp*			
			תִּכְתְּבוּ	*2mp*		כְּתַבְתֶּם	*2mp*		כּוֹתֵב	*ms*
			תִּכְתֹּֿבְנָה	*2fp*		כְּתַבְתֶּן	*2fp*		כּוֹתֶֿבֶת	*fs*
			יִכְתְּבוּ	*3mp*		כָּתְבוּ	*3cp*		כּוֹתְבִים	*mp*
			תִּכְתֹּֿבְנָה	*3fp*					כּוֹתְבוֹת	*fp*

Imperative			Future			Past				
									מ.ל.ך	
									rule	
מְלֹךְ	*ms*		אֶמְלֹךְ	*1cs*		מָלַֿכְתִּי	*1cs*			
מִלְכִי	*fs*		תִּמְלֹךְ	*2ms*		מָלַֿכְתָּ	*2ms*		**Infinitive**	
מִלְכוּ	*mp*		תִּמְלְכִי	*2fs*		מָלַכְתְּ	*2fs*		לִמְלֹךְ	
מְלֹֿכְנָה	*fp*		יִמְלֹךְ	*3ms*		מָלַךְ	*3ms*			
			תִּמְלֹךְ	*3fs*		מָלְכָה	*3fs*		**Present/ Participle**	
			נִמְלֹךְ	*1cp*		מָלַֿכְנוּ	*1cp*			
			תִּמְלְכוּ	*2mp*		מְלַכְתֶּם	*2mp*		מוֹלֵךְ	*ms*
			תִּמְלֹֿכְנָה	*2fp*		מְלַכְתֶּן	*2fp*		מוֹלֶֿכֶת	*fs*
			יִמְלְכוּ	*3mp*		מָלְכוּ	*3cp*		מוֹלְכִים	*mp*
			תִּמְלֹֿכְנָה	*3fp*					מוֹלְכוֹת	*fp*

Verb Charts, *continued*

מ.צ.א — *find*

Infinitive: לִמְצֹא

Imperative		Future		Past		Present/Participle	
מְצָא	ms	אֶמְצָא	1cs	מָצָאתִי	1cs		
מִצְאִי	fs	תִּמְצָא	2ms	מָצָאתָ	2ms		
מִצְאוּ	mp	תִּמְצְאִי	2fs	מָצָאת	2fs		
מְצֶאנָה	fp	יִמְצָא	3ms	מָצָא	3ms		
		תִּמְצָא	3fs	מָצְאָה	3fs		
		נִמְצָא	1cp	מָצָאנוּ	1cp	מוֹצֵא	ms
		תִּמְצְאוּ	2mp	מְצָאתֶם	2mp	מוֹצֵאת	fs
		תִּמְצֶאנָה	2fp	מְצָאתֶן	2fp	מוֹצְאִים	mp
		יִמְצְאוּ	3mp	מָצְאוּ	3cp	מוֹצְאוֹת	fp
		תִּמְצֶאנָה	3fp				

נ.ת.ן — *give, allow*

Infinitive: לָתֵת

Imperative		Future**		Past		Present/Participle	
תֵּן	ms*	אֶתֵּן	1cs	נָתַתִּי	1cs		
תְּנִי	fs	תִּתֵּן	2ms	נָתַתָּ	2ms		
תְּנוּ	mp	תִּתְּנִי	2fs	נָתַתְּ	2fs		
תֵּנָּה	fp	יִתֵּן	3ms	נָתַן	3ms		
		תִּתֵּן	3fs	נָתְנָה	3fs		
		נִתֵּן	1cp	נָתַנּוּ	1cp	נוֹתֵן	ms
		תִּתְּנוּ	2mp	נְתַתֶּם	2mp	נוֹתֶנֶת	fs
		תִּתֵּנָּה	2fp	נְתַתֶּן	2fp	נוֹתְנִים	mp
		יִתְּנוּ	3mp	נָתְנוּ	3cp	נוֹתְנוֹת	fp
		תִּתֵּנָּה	3fp				

*Alternate spelling: תְּנָה

**Many future tense forms have alternate spellings which are not shown here. This chart contains the most frequently used spellings in scripture.

Verb Charts, *continued*

Imperative		Future		Past		
						ס.ל.ח *forgive*
סְלַח	ms	אֶסְלַח	1cs	סָלַ֫חְתִּי	1cs	
סִלְחִי	fs	תִּסְלַח	2ms	סָלַ֫חְתָּ	2ms	
סִלְחוּ	mp	תִּסְלְחִי	2fs	סָלַ֫חַתְּ	2fs	**Infinitive**
סְלַ֫חְנָה	fp	יִסְלַח	3ms	סָלַח	3ms	לִסְלֹחַ
		תִּסְלַח	3fs	סָלְחָה	3fs	
		נִסְלַח	1cp	סָלַ֫חְנוּ	1cp	**Present/ Participle**
		תִּסְלְחוּ	2mp	סְלַחְתֶּם	2mp	סוֹלֵחַ ms
		תִּסְלַ֫חְנָה	2fp	סְלַחְתֶּן	2fp	סוֹלַ֫חַת fs
		יִסְלְחוּ	3mp	סָלְחוּ	3cp	סוֹלְחִים mp
		תִּסְלַ֫חְנָה	3fp			סוֹלְחוֹת fp

Imperative		Future		Past		
						ע.ז.ר *help, assist*
עֲזֹר	ms	אֶעֱזֹר	1cs	עָזַ֫רְתִּי	1cs	
עִזְרִי	fs	תַּעֲזֹר	2ms	עָזַ֫רְתָּ	2ms	
עִזְרוּ	mp	תַּעַזְרִי	2fs	עָזַרְתְּ	2fs	**Infinitive***
עֲזֹ֫רְנָה	fp	יַעֲזֹר	3ms	עָזַר	3ms	לַעֲזֹר
		תַּעֲזֹר	3fs	עָזְרָה	3fs	
		נַעֲזֹר	1cp	עָזַ֫רְנוּ	1cp	**Present/ Participle**
		תַּעַזְרוּ	2mp	עֲזַרְתֶּם	2mp	עוֹזֵר ms
		תַּעֲזֹ֫רְנָה	2fp	עֲזַרְתֶּן	2fp	עוֹזֶ֫רֶת fs
		יַעַזְרוּ	3mp	עָזְרוּ	3cp	עוֹזְרִים mp
		תַּעֲזֹ֫רְנָה	3fp			עוֹזְרוֹת fp

*The Biblical (archaic) spelling of the infinitive is shown in this chart. Its modern Hebrew spelling is לַעֲזֹר.

Verb Charts, *continued*

Imperative		Future		Past		
						ע.שׂ.ה
						make, do
עֲשֵׂה	*ms*	אֶעֱשֶׂה	*1cs*	עָשִׂ֫יתִי	*1cs*	
עֲשִׂי	*fs*	תַּעֲשֶׂה	*2ms*	עָשִׂ֫יתָ	*2ms*	
עֲשׂוּ	*mp*	תַּעֲשִׂי	*2fs*	עָשִׂית	*2fs*	**Infinitive**
עֲשֶׂ֫ינָה	*fp*	יַעֲשֶׂה	*3ms*	עָשָׂה	*3ms*	לַעֲשׂוֹת
		תַּעֲשֶׂה	*3fs*	עָשְׂתָה	*3fs*	
		נַעֲשֶׂה	*1cp*	עָשִׂ֫ינוּ	*1cp*	**Present/ Participle**
		תַּעֲשׂוּ	*2mp*	עֲשִׂיתֶם	*2mp*	עוֹשֶׂה *ms*
		תַּעֲשֶׂ֫ינָה	*2fp*	עֲשִׂיתֶן	*2fp*	עוֹשָׂה *fs*
		יַעֲשׂוּ	*3mp*	עָשׂוּ	*3cp*	עוֹשִׂים *mp*
		תַּעֲשֶׂ֫ינָה	*3fp*			עוֹשׂוֹת *fp*

Imperative		Future		Past		
						שׁ.ב.ת
						rest, cease, stop
שְׁבֹת	*ms*	אֶשְׁבֹּת	*1cs*	שָׁבַ֫תִּי	*1cs*	
שִׁבְתִּי	*fs*	תִּשְׁבֹּת	*2ms*	שָׁבַ֫תָּ	*2ms*	
שִׁבְתוּ	*mp*	תִּשְׁבְּתִי	*2fs*	שָׁבַתְּ	*2fs*	**Infinitive**
שְׁבֹ֫תְנָה	*fp*	יִשְׁבֹּת	*3ms*	שָׁבַת	*3ms*	לִשְׁבֹּת
		תִּשְׁבֹּת	*3fs*	שָׁבְתָה	*3fs*	
		נִשְׁבֹּת	*1cp*	שָׁבַ֫תְנוּ	*1cp*	**Present/ Participle**
		תִּשְׁבְּתוּ	*2mp*	שְׁבַתֶּם	*2mp*	שׁוֹבֵת *ms*
		תִּשְׁבֹּ֫תְנָה	*2fp*	שְׁבַתֶּן	*2fp*	שׁוֹבֶ֫תֶת *fs*
		יִשְׁבְּתוּ	*3mp*	שָׁבְתוּ	*3cp*	שׁוֹבְתִים *mp*
		תִּשְׁבֹּ֫תְנָה	*3fp*			שׁוֹבְתוֹת *fp*

Verb Charts, *continued*

Imperative		Future		Past			
						שׂ.מ.ח	
שְׂמַח	*ms*	אֶשְׂמַח	*1cs*	שָׂמַֽחְתִּי	*1cs*	*rejoice, be happy*	
שִׂמְחִי	*fs*	תִּשְׂמַח	*2ms*	שָׂמַֽחְתָּ	*2ms*		
שִׂמְחוּ	*mp*	תִּשְׂמְחִי	*2fs*	שָׂמַֽחַתְּ	*2fs*	**Infinitive**	
שְׂמַֽחְנָה	*fp*	יִשְׂמַח	*3ms*	שָׂמַח	*3ms*	לִשְׂמֹֽחַ	
		תִּשְׂמַח	*3fs*	שָׂמְחָה	*3fs*	**Present/ Participle**	
		נִשְׂמַח	*1cp*	שָׂמַֽחְנוּ	*1cp*	שָׂמֵֽחַ	*ms*
		תִּשְׂמְחוּ	*2mp*	שְׂמַחְתֶּם	*2mp*	שְׂמֵחָה	*fs*
		תִּשְׂמַֽחְנָה	*2fp*	שְׂמַחְתֶּן	*2fp*	שְׂמֵחִים	*mp*
		יִשְׂמְחוּ	*3mp*	שָׂמְחוּ	*3cp*	שְׂמֵחוֹת	*fp*
		תִּשְׂמַֽחְנָה	*3fp*				

Imperative		Future		Past			
						שׁ.מ.ע	
שְׁמַע	*ms*	אֶשְׁמַע	*1cs*	שָׁמַֽעְתִּי	*1cs*	*hear, heed*	
שִׁמְעִי	*fs*	תִּשְׁמַע	*2ms*	שָׁמַֽעְתָּ	*2ms*		
שִׁמְעוּ	*mp*	תִּשְׁמְעִי	*2fs*	שָׁמַֽעַתְּ	*2fs*	**Infinitive**	
שְׁמַֽעְנָה	*fp*	יִשְׁמַע	*3ms*	שָׁמַע	*3ms*	לִשְׁמֹֽעַ	
		תִּשְׁמַע	*3fs*	שָׁמְעָה	*3fs*	**Present/ Participle**	
		נִשְׁמַע	*1cp*	שָׁמַֽעְנוּ	*1cp*	שׁוֹמֵֽעַ	*ms*
		תִּשְׁמְעוּ	*2mp*	שְׁמַעְתֶּם	*2mp*	שׁוֹמַֽעַת	*fs*
		תִּשְׁמַֽעְנָה	*2fp*	שְׁמַעְתֶּן	*2fp*	שׁוֹמְעִים	*mp*
		יִשְׁמְעוּ	*3mp*	שָׁמְעוּ	*3cp*	שׁוֹמְעוֹת	*fp*
		תִּשְׁמַֽעְנָה	*3fp*				

Verb Charts, *continued*

Imperative		Future		Past		שׁ.מ.ר
שְׁמֹר	ms	אֶשְׁמֹר	1cs	שָׁמַ֫רְתִּי	1cs	*guard, keep*
שִׁמְרִי	fs	תִּשְׁמֹר	2ms	שָׁמַ֫רְתָּ	2ms	
שִׁמְרוּ	mp	תִּשְׁמְרִי	2fs	שָׁמַרְתְּ	2fs	**Infinitive**
שְׁמֹ֫רְנָה	fp	יִשְׁמֹר	3ms	שָׁמַר	3ms	לִשְׁמֹר
		תִּשְׁמֹר	3fs	שָׁמְרָה	3fs	**Present/ Participle**
		נִשְׁמֹר	1cp	שָׁמַ֫רְנוּ	1cp	שׁוֹמֵר ms
		תִּשְׁמְרוּ	2mp	שְׁמַרְתֶּם	2mp	שׁוֹמֶ֫רֶת fs
		תִּשְׁמֹ֫רְנָה	2fp	שְׁמַרְתֶּן	2fp	שׁוֹמְרִים mp
		יִשְׁמְרוּ	3mp	שָׁמְרוּ	3cp	שׁוֹמְרוֹת fp
		תִּשְׁמֹ֫רְנָה	3fp			

Glossary

For nouns and pronouns, the singular form of each Hebrew word is listed first, followed by the plural form wherever applicable. For adjectives and participles, only the masculine singular form is shown. This glossary contains all the words taught in *Messiah's Alphabet* Books 1 through 4.

א

father *m*	אָב, אָבוֹת
Abraham	אַבְרָהָם
lord, master *m*	אָדוֹן, אֲדוֹנִים
land, ground *f*	אֲדָמָה, אֲדָמוֹת
The Lord *m*	אֲדֹנָי
love	א.ה.ב
love *f*	אַהֲבָה
loving	אוֹהֵב
saying	אוֹמֵר
light *m*	אוֹר, אוֹרִים
sign *c*	אוֹת, אוֹתוֹת
one	אֶחָד
after, behind	אַחַר, אַחֲרֵי
there is no, there are no	אֵין
man *m*	אִישׁ, אֲנָשִׁים
to, towards	אֶל
these *c*	אֵלֶּה
God, gods *m*	אֱלֹהִים
mother *f*	אֵם, אִמָּהוֹת

א *continued*

say	א.מ.ר
truth *f*	אֱמֶת
we *c*	אֲנַחְנוּ, אָנוּ
I *c*	אָנֹכִי, אֲנִי
land, earth *f*	אֶרֶץ, אֲרָצוֹת
which, that, who	אֲשֶׁר, שֶׁ־
you *f*	אַתְּ, אַתֶּן
you *m*	אַתָּה, אַתֶּם

ב

in, with	בְּ־
choosing	בּוֹחֵר
trusting	בּוֹטֵחַ
creating	בּוֹרֵא
choose	ב.ח.ר
trust	ב.ט.ח
between, among	בֵּין
house *m*	בַּיִת, בָּתִּים
son *m*	בֵּן, בָּנִים

Glossary

morning *m*	בֹּקֶר , בְּקָרִים
create	ב.ר.א
in the beginning	בְּרֵאשִׁית
blessed	בָּרוּךְ
covenant *f*	בְּרִית
blessing *f*	בְּרָכָה , בְּרָכוֹת
daughter *f*	בַּת , בָּנוֹת

ג

redeem	ג.א.ל
redemption *f*	גְּאֻלָּה
mighty, strong	גִּבּוֹר
great, big	גָּדוֹל
greatness *f*	גְּדֻלָּה , גְּדוּלָה
nation, people *m*	גּוֹי , גּוֹיִם

ד

word, thing *m*	דָּבָר , דְּבָרִים
David	דָּוִד
generation *m*	דּוֹר , דּוֹרוֹת
road, way *c*	דֶּרֶךְ , דְּרָכִים

ה

the	הַ- , הֶ- , הָ- ,
he, it *m*	הוּא
walking, going	הוֹלֵךְ
she, it *f*	הִיא
be	ה.י.ה
today, the day	הַיּוֹם
walk, go	ה.ל.ך
they *m*	הֵם
they *f*	הֵן

ו

and..... *(may have other vowels under the vav)*	וְ- , וּ- ,

ז

this *f*	זֹאת
this *m*	זֶה
remembering	זוֹכֵר
remember	ז.כ.ר
memorial *m*	זֵכֶר
memorial *m*	זִכָּרוֹן , זִכְרוֹנוֹת
season, time *m*	זְמַן , זְמַנִּים
seed, offspring *m*	זֶרַע

Glossary

ח

festival *m*	חַג, חַגִּים
new	חָדָשׁ
sin	ח.ט.א
sin *m*	חֵטְא, חֲטָאִים
life *m*	חַיִּים
grace, favor *m*	חֵן
kindness, mercy *m*	חֶסֶד, חֲסָדִים

ט

good	טוֹב

י

hand *f*	יָד, יָדַיִם
know	י.ד.ע
day *m*	יוֹם, יָמִים
forming	יוֹצֵר
Jacob	יַעֲקֹב
Isaac	יִצְחָק
exodus *f*	יְצִיאָה, יְצִיאוֹת
form	י.צ.ר
awe, fear *f*	יִרְאָה

י
continued

sit, dwell	י.שׁ.ב
Yeshua, Jesus	יֵשׁוּעַ
Israel	יִשְׂרָאֵל

כ

like, as	כְּ–
honor, glory *m*	כָּבוֹד
that, because	כִּי
strength, ability *m*	כֹּחַ
all, every	כֹּל, כָּל
bow, bend the knee	כ.ר.ע
write	כ.ת.ב

ל

for, to	לְ–
no, not	לֹא
Leah	לֵאָה
heart *m*	לֵב, לֵבָב, לְבָבוֹת
bread, food *m*	לֶחֶם
night *m*	לַיְלָה, לֵילוֹת
for the sake of	לְמַעַן

Glossary

ל *continued*

forever and ever .... לְעוֹלָם וָעֶד

in front of, before .... לִפְנֵי

מ

from .... מִ־, מִן

shield, defender *m* .... מָגֵן, מָגִנִּים

what? how? .... מַה, מֶה, מָה

quickly .... מְהֵרָה, בִּמְהֵרָה

ruling, reigning .... מוֹלֵךְ

doorpost *f* .... מְזוּזָה, מְזוּזוֹת

forgive, pardon .... מ.ח.ל

who? .... מִי

angel, messenger *m*. מַלְאָךְ, מַלְאָכִים

work, task *f* ... מְלָאכָה, מְלָאכוֹת

rule, reign .... מ.ל.ךְ

king *m* .... מֶלֶךְ, מְלָכִים

kingdom *f* .... מַלְכוּת, מַלְכֻיּוֹת

from .... מִן, מִ־

Egypt .... מִצְרַיִם

deed, act *m* ..... מַעֲשֶׂה, מַעֲשִׂים

מ *continued*

find .... מ.צ.א

commandment *f* ...... מִצְוָה, מִצְוֹת

place *m* .... מָקוֹם, מְקוֹמוֹת

Moses .... מֹשֶׁה

anointed (one), Messiah *m* .... מָשִׁיחַ

family *f* .. מִשְׁפָּחָה, מִשְׁפָּחוֹת

נ

faithful .... נֶאֱמָן

prophet *m* .... נָבִיא, נְבִיאִים

awesome .... נוֹרָא

giving .... נוֹתֵן

Noah .... נֹחַ

soul *f* .... נֶפֶשׁ, נְפָשׁוֹת

breath, spirit *f* .... נְשָׁמָה, נְשָׁמוֹת

give .... נ.ת.ן

ס

forgive .... ס.ל.ח

book *m* .... סֵפֶר, סְפָרִים

Glossary

ע

servant, slave *m* .... עֶבֶד, עֲבָדִים

as far as, until, up to .... עַד

eternity, world *m* .... עוֹלָם, עוֹלָמִים

making, doing .... עוֹשֶׂה

strength *m* .... עֹז

help .... ע.ז.ר

help *f* .... עֶזְרָה

eye *f* .... עַיִן, עֵינַיִם

city *f* .... עִיר, עָרִים

upon, about, above, on .... עַל

with .... עִם

people, nation *m* .... עַם, עַמִּים

evening *m* .... עֶרֶב, עַרְבִּים

make, do .... ע.שׂ.ה

time *f* .... עֵת

פ

face *m* .... פָּנִים

fruit *m* .... פְּרִי

צ

host, multitude *m* ..... צָבָא, צְבָאוֹת

righteousness *f* .... צְדָקָה

rock *m* .... צוּר, צוּרִים

Zion .... צִיוֹן

trouble, distress *f* ..... צָרָה, צָרוֹת

ק

holy .... קָדוֹשׁ

holiness *f* .... קְדוּשָׁה

holiness *m* .... קֹדֶשׁ

voice, sound *m* .... קוֹל

ר

head *m* .... רֹאשׁ, רָאשִׁים

much, many, abundant .... רַב

Rebecca .... רִבְקָה

spirit, wind *f* .... רוּחַ

Rachel .... רָחֵל

mercy, compassion *m* .... רַחֲמִים

evil, bad .... רַע

Glossary

will, acceptance, favor, *m* .... רָצוֹן

wicked, evil .... רָשָׁע

שׁ

which, that, who .... שֶׁ־

rest, cease working .... שׁ.ב.ת

sabbath *f* .... שַׁבָּת,   שַׁבָּתוֹת

guarding, keeping .... שׁוֹמֵר

of .... שֶׁל

peace *m* .... שָׁלוֹם

name *m* .... שֵׁם,   שֵׁמוֹת

rejoice .... שׂ.מ.ח

happiness, joy *f* .. שִׂמְחָה,   שְׂמָחוֹת

heaven, heavens, sky *m* .... שָׁמַיִם

hear, heed, listen .... שׁ.מ.ע

guard, keep................................ שׁ.מ.ר

year *f*................. שָׁנָה,   שָׁנִים

gate *m* .... שַׁעַר,   שְׁעָרִים

Sarah .... שָׂרָה

ת

instruction, Torah, law *f* .... תּוֹרָה

always, continually .... תָּמִיד

glory *f*................................... תִּפְאֶרֶת

prayer *f*............. תְּפִלָּה,   תְּפִלּוֹת

23590036R00094

Printed in Great Britain
by Amazon